NOVEMBER

A MONTH OF IDEAS AT YOUR FINGERTIPS!

PRESCHOOL– KINDERGARTEN

WRITTEN BY

Deborah Burleson, Ada Hanley Goren, Lucia Kemp Henry, Jean Huff, Mackie Rhodes, Valerie SchifferDanoff, Jan Trautman, Amy Zierow

EDITED BY

Lynn Bemer Coble, Ada Hanley Goren, Mackie Rhodes, Jennifer Rudisill, Karen P. Shelton, Gina Sutphin

ILLUSTRATED BY

Jennifer Tipton Bennett, Cathy Spangler Bruce, Pam Crane, Clevell Harris, Lucia Kemp Henry, Susan Hodnett, Sheila Krill, Rebecca Saunders, Barry Slate, Donna K. Teal

COVER DESIGNED BY

Jennifer Tipton Bennett

©1996 by THE EDUCATION CENTER, INC.
All rights reserved except as here noted.

ISBN# 1-56234-133-2

Manufactured in the United States
10 9 8 7 6 5 4 3

TABLE OF CONTENTS

November Calendar

International Drum Month

Get with the beat! November is International Drum Month! Invite a local drummer to demonstrate how he plays his drums during a visit to your class. Or ask your school's music teacher to show pictures of different types of drums and play recordings of the sounds made by each one. Encourage your little ones to keep cadence using their own drums created from margarine containers with lids.

Cat Week—Begins First Sunday In November

Celebrate our feline friend, the cat, during this week. Invite youngsters who have pet cats to bring pictures of their cats to class. Encourage them to tell the other students some interesting things about their cats. Then have each student make a cat mask. Cut out the center of a paper plate for each child. Have him decorate the rim of the plate to resemble a cat's head, gluing on construction-paper ears and whiskers as desired. When the cat masks have been completed, divide students into groups of three. Encourage each group to hold their masks in front of their faces and recite "The Three Little Kittens."

1—National Authors' Day

Honor an author today. Gather several books written by a popular children's author. Display the books in the class reading center. Explain to youngsters that an author is someone who makes up the stories in books. Select one of the books to read aloud. Show and tell the students the name of the author. After reading the story, invite each child to complete the statement, "If I were an author, I would write a story about _____."

3—First Automobile Show

On this date in 1900, the first automobile show was held at Madison Square Garden in New York City. To commemorate this special event, have a class automobile show. Ask each student to bring a toy model or photograph of a car to class. Label each child's toy or photo with his name; then have him write or dictate a sentence about his car. To set up the automobile show, display the cars and sentences on a table with the title, "Crazy About Cars!" Invite parents and other classes to visit the car show.

3—First Animal In Space

In 1957 a dog named Laika was the first animal to travel into space in a spacecraft. Invite students to imagine that all kinds of animals have traveled and lived in space. If the class were to take a space trip, what animals would they see? Give each child a sheet of white construction paper. Encourage him to draw a picture of an animal he might see while in space. Label each child's drawing with his dictation; then display all the pictures on a bulletin board titled "Animals In Space."

6—Birthdate Of John Philip Sousa

John Philip Sousa—"The March King"—was born on this day in 1854. He is well known for his many march compositions, including "The Stars and Stripes Forever." Obtain a recording of this or any other march. Invite youngsters to line up; then turn on the music and have them march around the room to celebrate the talents of this great man!

21—World Hello Day

Encourage youngsters to take time today to say "Hello" to one another. Begin by playing the song "Say Hello" from *Kidding Around With Greg And Steve* (Youngheart Records). Afterward provide each child with a crayon and a sheet of paper programmed with "Hello" across the top. Explain that each child will greet another child, then ask that child to sign his name on the paper. Challenge the children to obtain at least ten different signatures in this manner. Encourage students to take their papers home, then greet family members and have them add their signatures to the list.

24—Americans View Lion For First Time

During an exhibition in Boston, Massachusetts in 1716, Americans saw a lion for the first time on this day. Explain to youngsters that not all lions live in captivity. Their natural habitats are in woodlands and grassy plains where they can find food and water. Tell students that you are going to read a story about a girl who searches for a lion in its natural habitat. Then read aloud *Nanta's Lion* by Suse MacDonald (Morrow Junior Books). Encourage the students to look carefully for the lion as you read the story. Invite them to roar when they see the lion.

National Game And Puzzle Week— Last Week In November

Puzzled over what to do with youngsters this week? Solve that problem by setting up game and puzzle centers to celebrate these nationally recognized activities. Each day provide a different game and puzzle for each center. Invite small groups of youngsters to take turns visiting the centers so that every group has the opportunity to use each center.

November

CLASSROOM NEWS

Teacher: _____ Date: _____

A Peek At The Week

Looking Ahead

Reminders

Help Wanted

Special Thanks

Alphabet Soup

Serve your little ones a healthy portion of activities from this potluck mixture of alphabet soup!

—by Mackie Rhodes

"Alpha-Noodle" Soup

Youngsters will get a healthy serving of upper- and lowercase letter matching with this fun water table activity! From the bottoms of Styrofoam® plates or meat trays, cut 26 1" x 2" rectangles to represent noodles. Using a permanent marker, write a different lowercase letter on each Styrofoam® noodle so that all the letters are represented. If desired, write the same letter on both sides of each noodle. Underline letters that may be easily confused with one another, such as *d* and *p*. Inside the bowls of 26 plastic spoons, write a different uppercase letter. Place the spoons on a tray near the water table. To make the soup, partially fill the water table with water; then put the Styrofoam® noodles in. To play, have a child select a spoon, then use it to scoop the noodle with the corresponding lowercase letter. Ready for some fun? Soup's on!

Harvesttime

Students will reap bundles of recognition and visual-discrimination skills with this letter-harvesting activity. From construction paper, cut a supply of leaves and garden vegetables. Label some vegetable cutouts with letters and others with geometric forms or figures resembling letters. Laminate them; then attach each leaf and vegetable cutout to a craft stick. To make a garden, poke the sticks of several leaves into a mound of play dough. Then add some vegetables to the mound. In turn, encourage each child to pick only the vegetables labeled with letters from the garden. Then have him name the letters. It's harvesttime!

Frozen Letters

Make a frozen alphabet to give your little ones a chilling tactile experience during water play. Nearly fill a set of letter sand molds with water. Place the molds on cookie sheets; then freeze them. After putting water in your class water table, add each frozen letter mold to the water. The children will delight in the opportunity to remove the iced letters from the molds, mix them around in the water, and then match them again to their original molds. As they manipulate the ice and molds, encourage the students to name each letter. During this activity, engage students in a discussion about melting ice and the interesting forms the ice letters assume as they melt. It's a chilling, but educational, experience!

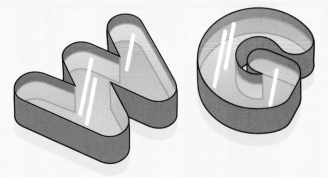

In A Fog

These letters may be in a fog, but your little ones will have no trouble seeing them clearly. Holding a small mirror faceup, encourage a child to breathe through his mouth onto the surface to make it foggy. Then have him use his finger to write a named letter. When the surface clears, repeat the procedure naming a different letter. Before the mirror is passed to the next child, wipe it clean with a disinfectant solution.

Jack Frost

Jack Frost is the perfect visitor to help freeze letter recognition into the memories of your little ones. Using a piece of tagboard and glitter, make a child-sized crown. From white construction paper, cut out icicle shapes. Label each with a different letter of the alphabet. Laminate the icicles; then use a hole puncher to make a hole in the top of each. Thread a length of yarn through the hole, and tie the ends together to make a necklace. Assign one child to be Jack Frost. Have that child wear the crown. Have each of the other children wear an icicle necklace. To play, have all the children stand straight, tall, and stiff as if they are icicles. With his back turned to the icicles, instruct Jack Frost to say, "I command letter ___ to freeze. All others melt as you please." The child wearing the icicle with the named letter will remain frozen while the other children pretend to melt to the ground. Encourage Jack Frost to check for the correctness of the letter on the remaining frozen icicle. Then have that child take a turn playing Jack Frost. Continue the game until every child has had an opportunity to be Jack Frost.

Surprise Boxes

This boxed set of letters will provide youngsters with the perfect measure of surprise to motivate them in letter-recognition and sound-association practice. Collect a set of five or more lidded boxes graduated in size so that they can be nested together. Cover the boxes and lids with Con-Tact® paper. From construction paper, cut a set of letters and laminate them. Place a letter inside the smallest box. Then, on the back of a different letter cutout, place a piece of rolled tape so that the cutout can be attached to a box lid. Tape one letter to each lid. Then nest the boxes together. During a group time, pass the set of boxes to a student. Ask him to name the letter on the lid, then say a word that begins with that letter. Have him remove the lid and take the next box out to pass to the next child. As each child receives the set of boxes, encourage him to do the same. When the smallest box is received, have that child remove its lid, then pass the letter inside to the next child. To play again, ask the students to remove the letters from the lids. Prepare the boxes using different letters; then have the children continue passing the box set around the group.

For variety at another time, use pictures of items that begin with different letters of the alphabet. As each child receives a box, have him name the picture on the lid and the letter with which it begins.

Letter Legacy

Have your youngsters prepare this alphabet quilt to enjoy now, then to leave as their legacy for next year's incoming class. Cut 56 sheets of colored construction paper into nine-inch squares. Give each child two squares. Have every child select a different letter of the alphabet so that each letter is represented. On the first sheet of paper, help the child write his letter. Then encourage him to decorate the letter with colored markers. On the other sheet, have the child cut and glue magazine pictures of that letter and objects beginning with that letter. Invite students to sign their names on one of any of the four remaining sheets of paper. Laminate each sheet. Using a hole puncher, cut five evenly-spaced holes along each edge of each sheet. In a spacious area, alphabetically arrange the papers so that eight sheets make up each row and each letter page precedes its corresponding picture page. On the bottom row, position the four signature sheets after the last picture sheet. Assemble the quilt by lacing the sheets together with ribbon or yarn. If desired, lace a ribbon through the top holes of the quilt and around a six-foot-long sash rod for ease of hanging. Display the class quilt in a prominent place for all to learn from and enjoy.

Alphabet Rope Hunt

Give youngsters a different way to get through the alphabet—blindfolded! Along the way, they will get practice in reciting the alphabet as well as practice in one-to-one correspondence. Using an X-acto® knife, cut a small hole from each of the centers of 26 large plastic lids. On the inside of each lid, use a permanent marker to write a different letter of the alphabet. Slip the lids onto a length of rope in alphabetical order; then tie the rope between two sturdy supports, such as a built-in cabinet and a large wooden desk. Spread the lids out along the rope. To play, assign each child a letter. Blindfold him or ask him to close his eyes. Invite the child to recite the alphabet as he moves alongside the rope, feeling for a lid to correspond to each named letter. Encourage him to continue until he names his assigned letter. Ask him to hold on to that lid as you remove his blindfold. Then have him check the letter on that lid to see if it is printed with his assigned letter. If not, ask him to name the letter on that lid, then find the lid with his assigned letter.

Attractive Letters

Looking for a letter-formation activity with lots of magnetic appeal for youngsters? Then attract their attention with this activity. Using colored magnetic counting chips, encourage a child to form upper- or lowercase letters. Then with the wave of a magnetic wand over the letters, have her collect the chips and start again.

g-g-g-g-g-g-g-g

Little Roadsters

Rev up your youngsters' sound-to-letter association skills with this speedy little learning activity. Make the large plastic letter lids as described in "Alphabet Rope Hunt." (Cutting the hole in the middle of the lids is not necessary.) These will represent steering wheels for this activity. Set up an obstacle course to represent a roadway. For example, use a balance beam for a bridge, a box with the flaps folded in for a tunnel, a large plastic cone for a tree, and a Hula-Hoop® for a lake. Near the beginning of the course, arrange sets of up to ten steering wheels so that the letters are visible. Explain the sequence of the course to your students. Then have a child select the steering wheel printed with a named letter. Invite that student to pretend to be a race car driver. With the steering wheel held in front of him, encourage him to maneuver through the obstacle course as if driving a car. As he drives, suggest he use the sound his letter makes to produce an engine noise. For instance, if his steering wheel has the letter *G,* encourage him to say "g-g-g-g-g-g-g." Give every child an opportunity to drive the course. Start your engines! Go!

Yellow Brick Road

Little ones will love following this alphabet yellow brick road to reach the surprise at the end. In a decorated shoebox, place small plastic prizes and stickers. Then on each of 26 sheets of yellow construction paper, write a different letter. Laminate the sheets. Tape the sheets in place as you alphabetically arrange them into a spiral path on the floor, having the letter *A* begin the spiral at the center and the letter *Z* complete the spiral at the outside. Put the box of prizes at the end of the spiral, next to the letter *Z.* Encourage each child to take a turn following the yellow brick road from *A* to *Z.* Have him name each letter as he steps on its corresponding brick. When he reaches the end of the road, have him open the box and select a prize to keep. Just follow the yellow brick road to alphabet learning.

Bottom's Up Letter Cups

Promote initial-sound and letter associations using these letter cups. With a permanent marker, write a different upper- or lowercase letter on the bottom of each of 26 paper cups. Collect small toys and objects that begin with a sound for each letter of the alphabet. When each letter is represented by an object, prepare this activity.

On a large table, randomly arrange the items with space enough to put cups over them. With bottoms up, alphabetically place the cups on the floor or another table several feet away from the item table. Encourage youngsters to take turns finding a cup with a named letter. Then have each student take his cup to the item table to find the object that begins with the letter on his cup. Have him place the cup over that item, then return to his seat. In turn, have the other students do likewise, until all of the items have been covered with a cup. Then, to extend the activity, reverse the procedure. Have a student remove the cup of a given letter and return it to its original place. Encourage the students to alphabetize the cups as they are replaced.

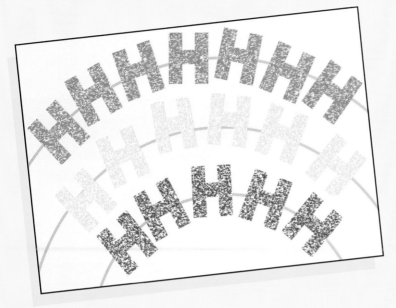

A Rainbow-Letter Day

Here's a rainy-day activity that will add color to indoor letter study. On each of a classroom quantity of large sheets of construction paper, draw several arcs to represent a rainbow. To represent several colors of the rainbow, pour different colors of paint into separate trays. Provide letter sponges to represent the current letter being studied. Using the sponges, encourage youngsters to make prints of that letter on the arcs of their rainbows. When the paintings are completed and dried, hang them with the title "A Rainbow-Letter Day."

"Alpha-Band"

Youngsters will rock to the rhythm of the alphabet when they create their own unique letter instruments. Using a die cutter, cut each letter of the alphabet from construction paper. Provide a variety of craft supplies, cardboard tubes, small containers, rice, beans, small bells, and other miscellaneous objects. Have each child select items to create a noisemaking instrument. Assist him in designing and making his instrument. Then assign a letter of the alphabet to that child. Attach that letter cutout to his instrument. After all the instruments are completed and every letter is represented, sing a round of the "Alphabet Song." As each letter is sung, encourage the child with the corresponding instrument to play along. Before long, your "alpha-band" will be ready to go on the road!

Hand Stacking

This hand-stacking game will become a hands-down favorite when it comes to practicing alphabet sequencing and left-right discrimination! Have each student select a partner. Sitting at a table, have one child place a hand down on the table and say, *"A"* to begin the sequence of the alphabet. Invite his partner to gently place his hand over the first child's hand and say, *"B."* Then guide the first child to place his other hand on the hand stack and name the next letter. Have his partner do likewise. When each child has placed both of his hands on the stack, have the child with his hand on the bottom move that hand to the top of the stack. Encourage the partners to continue in this manner until they have stacked their hands to the entire alphabet. At the end of the game, have the child with the hand at the top of the stack tell whether his right or left hand is on top.

11

Muffin Tins

You don't need the muffin man—just a muffin tin—to make these muffin-tin prints to use for letter-writing practice. To begin, pour white paint into a tray. Provide a large sheet of dark construction paper for each child. Using a sponge dipped into the paint, have each child spread paint over the top of a regular or mini muffin tin. Starting at the top of his paper, have the child turn the muffin tin over and press it onto the paper to make a tin print. Then have him make another set of prints below the first. After the paint dries, supply colored markers. Starting at the top left side of the paper, encourage each child to write the letter of the week in each circle. Have him follow a left-to-right and top-to-bottom progression as he fills in the circles.

Shopping Trip

Your little shoppers will load their baskets with auditory-memory and letter-recognition skills with this shopping exercise. To prepare, use a die cutter to cut six sets of the letters of the alphabet. Provide a basket for the children's use. From each alphabet set, remove the same six letters; then randomly arrange these letters on a table. Explain to students that they will play a listening game. Have one child select a letter from the table to put in the basket. After she makes her selection, guide her to say, "I went shopping and bought an ___," filling in the blank with the name of the selected letter. Then have her pass the basket to the next student. Have that student select the same letter as the first child *and* a different letter of her choice. Encourage her to repeat the sentence and add the name of her chosen letter. In turn, have students proceed in this manner, adding a new letter to the sequence on each turn, until a child incorrectly recalls the sequence. Replace the letters and have that child start the game over. Continue to play until every child has had the opportunity to participate. Further challenge students' memory and recognition abilities by periodically changing the sets of letters.

"Sew" Pretty Alphabet

Students will learn some of the fundamentals of sewing while making these letters for display. Purchase thirteen 10 1/2" x 13 1/2" plastic needlepoint canvases. Cut each canvas in half. Smooth the edges of each canvas by trimming away any excess plastic. Using a permanent marker, trace or draw the outline of a large block letter onto each canvas so that every letter of the alphabet is represented. Have each child select a canvas letter to sew. Provide him with a blunt plastic needle threaded with an arm-length piece of yarn. Demonstrate how to insert and pull the needle through the canvas to create stitches. Encourage the child to fill in the area outlined by the letter with stitches, reassuring him that any stitch length is acceptable. Invite him to work on his letter during transitions and quiet times. Replace the yarn in the needle as necessary. When all the letters are complete, display them as the class alphabet chart. It's an alphabet that's "sew" pretty!

Letter Press

You'll be quite impressed with your youngsters' letter formation skills in this multisensory activity. Supply each child with some play dough to shape into a patty. Encourage him to form letters in the dough by making imprints with small, textured objects such as snap-together blocks, spools, bottle tops, and pasta shapes. Letters with unusual and interesting patterns will appear. Impressive!

License Plate

Did you get the license on that car? Youngsters will need a quick eye, a sharp memory, and a fast pen to track down speeding cars in this dramatic-play activity. To prepare, use scissors to round the corners on a supply of 9" x 12" white construction paper. With a marker, write a three-, four-, or five-letter sequence on each sheet. Embellish each to resemble a license plate; then laminate them.

To play, provide students with pads of paper and writing utensils, and encourage them to role-play police officers. If desired, have available police badges and hats. Invite one child to be the speeding car. Using a spring-type clothespin, attach one license plate to the back of his shirt. Have the car position himself so that the police officers can see the license plate on his back. Suggest that the officers concentrate on the license and try to remember all the letters in the same sequence as they appear. After a brief time, give the signal, "Go." Have the car speed away to park in an area with his back away from the officers. Next encourage the police officers to write the letters from the license plate onto their pads. When they finish, have the car speed back around to park in front of the officers. Have each officer compare the letters written on his pad to the car's license plate. If he remembered and wrote the license-plate letters correctly, invite that officer to give the car a ticket—the paper with the license written on it. Then continue play, giving each child a turn to be the speeding car.

Bug Brigade

This alphabet bug brigade will provide many opportunities for your youngsters to practice tactical maneuvers in letter recognition, letter sequencing, and lowercase-to-uppercase matching. Using a die cutter, cut each upper- and lowercase letter of the alphabet from laminated construction paper. On each of 26 large pompoms, hot-glue a different uppercase letter. Do the same with 26 slightly smaller pom-poms and the lowercase letters. To each letter pom-pom, add wiggle eyes and pipe-cleaner antennae and legs to create bugs, as desired. To use the alphabet bug brigade, have students alphabetically sequence the bugs, play a letter recognition game, or pair the upper- and lowercase letter bugs together.

Alphabet Boa

Share this slithery, slinky snake with your youngsters for scads of letter-learning fun! To make an alphabet boa, cut a length of sturdy 2 1/2-inch-wide, or wider, craft ribbon. Round off the left end of the ribbon; then hot-glue large wiggle eyes and a red felt tongue onto it. Purchase or make a set of felt letters. Along the length of the ribbon center, hot-glue 26 short pieces of Velcro® (hook side up). To use the snake, challenge students to place the felt letters along its body in correct sequence. For a variation, place letters on the snake, leaving some letters off at random; then ask students to identify the missing letters. To extend alphabet learning, place the boa with letters attached in the dress-up area. Encourage students to incorporate this versatile learning object into their dramatic-play schemes. S-s-simply s-s-super learning!

Parachute

Delight will fill the air as youngsters play this letter-recognition game. On a purchased class parachute, cover the center hole with paper and tape. (If a parachute is not available, use a large bedsheet instead.) In a spacious area, spread out the parachute. Place a set of alphabet sponges in the center of the parachute. Explain to students that they will shake the parachute to make it appear to float in the air. Then, when you call out an action word, they will gently place the parachute on the floor and perform the named action once around the parachute. To play, have the students surround and hold on to the edges of the parachute. As the children shake the parachute, the sponge letters will bounce around at random. After a short interval of time, call out an action word, such as "jump" or "skip." When each student completes the action and returns to his original position, have him pick up the sponge letter closest to him. Encourage each child to show and name his letter.

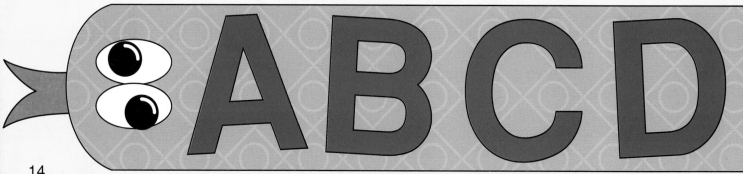

Letter "Scent-sation"

This letter-of-the-week activity will create a real "scent-sation" with your little ones. Fill several saltshakers with flavored gelatin powder. Provide a sheet of dark construction paper for each child. Assist him as needed in writing the upper- and lowercase letters of the week. Then have him paint glue over his letters. Using a shaker of gelatin, encourage the child to cover his letters with the powder. When the letters are dry, display them on a bulletin board entitled "Letter 'Scent-sation.' "

Inchworm

Little ones will love inching their way through the alphabet with this familiar game of cooperation and skill. Have your students form a line, standing with their legs apart. Ask them to leave enough room to stretch their arms out and touch the person in front of them. Explain that they are going to be an inchworm that moves to the letters of the alphabet. Give the first student a ball. Have him pass the ball between his legs to the student behind him. As the ball is passed, the first child will say, *"A."* Then have the second student pass the ball over his head to the next student while saying, *"B."* In turn, have the third student pass the ball between his legs, naming the next letter of the alphabet. Encourage the students to continue in this manner until the entire alphabet has been recited. If you run out of children before letters, simply have all the children turn and face the opposite direction; then continue to pass the ball in the same manner as before. The ups and downs of saying the alphabet have never been more fun!

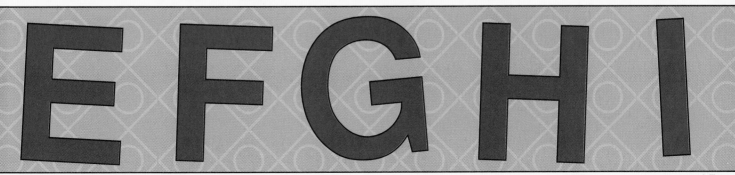

Light-Filtered Letters

Illuminate youngsters' letter-recognition skills with this light-filtering activity. For each child, supply a folded dark bath towel and a sheet of dark construction paper with a large chalk letter printed on it. Have each child place the paper on the towel. Using a blunt pencil point, have her punch holes along the lines of her letter by pressing the point through the paper. Then turn the classroom lights down. Holding her paper in front of her so the class can see, encourage each child to shine a flashlight at the paper from behind. Ask the children to identify the letter by looking at the shape made by the lighted dots. Afterwards, for an enlightening display, hang the letters in the classroom windows.

Signs Of The Alphabet

Promote the exploration of other means of symbolic language by teaching the hand signs that correspond to each letter being studied. Laminate the "Alphabet Hand Signs" charts on pages 19 and 20; then keep them available and visible in your classroom. Periodically encourage your children to practice making the hand symbol for each new or review letter. Youngsters may surprise you with the inventive and creative ways they combine signs to communicate. And you will be delighted with the additional opportunities to provide finger-manipulation practice for students!

Fancy Footwork

On a warm day, try this outdoor activity to help reinforce letter knowledge and formation. In advance, send a note to parents explaining that their children will be making paint footprints. Encourage them to have their children dress appropriately. To prepare for the activity, cut several lengths of white bulletin-board paper. Using a permanent marker, write a series of upper- or lowercase letters, with each letter large enough to fill the paper from top to bottom. Take the paper, a dishpan of water, a supply of towels, washable paint, and a large shallow paint tray outdoors with you. Spread the bulletin-board paper over the ground. Pour a thin layer of paint into the tray. Invite each child, in turn, to step barefoot into the tray of paint. Then encourage him to walk along a letter on the paper, leaving a footprint letter when finished. Have him rinse and dry his feet. When the footprint letters are dry, display them in your classroom or school hallway with the title "Fancy Footwork."

Muddy Worms

How can a scoop of mud and squirmy worms be used to learn letter formations? Find out with this sweet sensory activity that will have your students manipulating worms into letters and changing their "yucks" into "yums." For each child, provide a large disposable plastic plate and a spoon. Place a dollop of chocolate whipped topping on each plate to represent mud. Then give each child several Gummy Worms®. Encourage him to spread the mud over his plate, then to use the worms to form letters in it. After experimenting with letter formations, invite the students to eat their mud and worms. Squish, squirm, gulp! Mud, worms, and the alphabet are a yummy combination!

Water Magic

A spray bottle and some large sheets of paper are all that are needed for warm-weather letter-formation fun. To prepare, cut several lengths of dark bulletin-board paper. Then fill several bottles that have adjustable spray nozzles with water. Hang the sheets of paper outdoors on a fence or brick wall. Pair students; then provide one student in the pair with the spray bottle. As his partner calls out a letter, encourage him to use the spray bottle to write that letter on the paper. Like magic, the letters will begin to disappear as the water dries on the paper; then new letters can be written. Have the students in each pair take turns calling out and writing letters. What wonderfully wet alphabet fun!

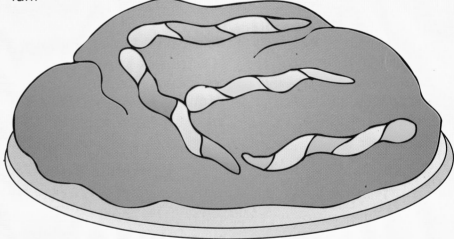

Tossing Around the Alphabet

Watch your youngsters catch the letter-recognition fever when you toss these alphabet balls their way. Label each of 26 foam balls with a different letter of the alphabet. After forming a large circle, have the children toss the balls at random to one another until given a signal. On the signal, ask each child to catch and hold a ball. Taking turns around the circle, have each child name the letter on his ball. Give another signal to begin play again.

Hall Pass

Reinforce letter recognition with the use of letter-of-the-week helper cards and hall passes. On several 4" x 6" cards, write the letter of the week. Embellish the cards with stickers or pictures of items that begin with that letter; then laminate them. Using a hole puncher, make a hole in each top corner. Tie the end of a length of yarn through each hole. Have your daily helpers wear the cards or use them as hall passes.

Hand Shadows

There's not a shadow of a doubt that problem solving will be made fun in this letter formation activity using hand shadows. Set up an overhead projector to face a blank wall. With the light on, challenge students to use their hands and arms to make shadows of named letters. To turn this activity into a game of charades, whisper a letter name into a child's ear. As that child forms the letter using his hand shadows, have the other children try to guess the letter. Allow the first child to guess correctly to have the next turn.

Healthy Letters

This letter-perfect idea can make a healthy snack both fun and educational. Provide a letter-shaped cookie cutter to represent the letter currently being studied. Give each child a slice of cheese and two slices of bread. Using the cookie cutter, have her cut the letter from her cheese and bread. Encourage her to assemble the letters into a sandwich before eating them. Mmmm, good!

Alphabet Books

Alphabatics
Written by Suse MacDonald
Published by Bradbury Press

*Eating The Alphabet: Fruits And
    Vegetables From A To Z*
Written by Lois Ehlert
Published by Harcourt Brace, Publishers

Chicka Chicka Boom Boom
Written by Bill Martin, Jr., and John Archambault
Published by Simon & Schuster Inc.

Anno's Alphabet: An Adventure In Imagination
Illustrated by Mitsumasa Anno
Published by Harper & Row, Publishers

Alpha Bugs: A Pop-Up Alphabet
Written by David A. Carter
Published by Little Simon

Old Black Fly
Written by Jim Aylesworth
Published by Henry Holt & Company, Inc.

Handsigns: A Sign Language Alphabet
Illustrated by Kathleen Fain
Published by Chronicle Books

Action Alphabet
Written and Illustrated by Marty Neumeier
    and Byron Glaser
Published by Greenwillow Books

Have You Ever Seen...? An ABC Book
Written by Beau Gardner
Published by BGA Publishing, Inc.

The Z Was Zapped: A Play In Twenty-Six Acts
Written by Chris Van Allsburg
Published by Houghton Mifflin Company

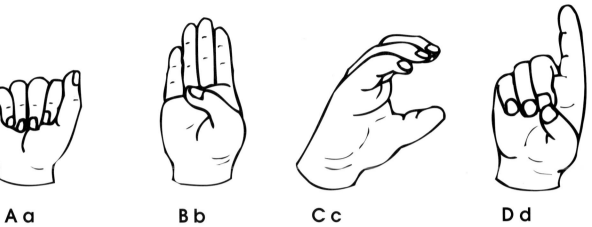

A a   B b   C c   D d

E e   F f   G g   H h

   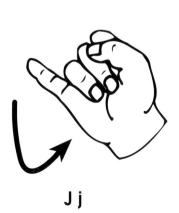      

I i   J j   K k   L l

Alphabet Hand Signs

Use with "Signs Of The Alphabet" on page 16.

 **M m**

 N n

 **O o**

 **P p**

 **Q q**

 **R r**

 **S s**

 **T t**

 **U u**

 **V v**

W w

X x

 **Y y**

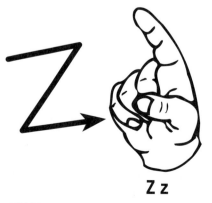 **Z z**

PASS THE PEANUT BUTTER

Spread the news—November is Peanut Butter Lovers' Month! Whether your youngsters are fans of crunchy or creamy, with jelly or without, they'll love these activities about America's favorite food!

ideas contributed by Jean Huff and Ada Hanley Goren

AN ODE TO PEANUT BUTTER

Invite your little ones to sing the praises of peanut butter with this familiar tune.

Peanut Butter In A Jar
(sung to the tune of "Twinkle, Twinkle Little Star")

Peanut butter in a jar,
Peanut-butter candy bar.
Peanut butter, smooth and sweet,
Or a crunchy, nutty treat.
Peanut butter on my bread,
How I love that yummy spread!

PAM CRANE

PEANUTS OR PEANUT BUTTER?

Youngsters will learn how peanut butter is made when you read the big book *From Peanuts To Peanut Butter* by Melvin Berger, published by Newbridge Communications, Inc. (This book can be ordered directly from Newbridge at 1-800-867-0307.) Note that the child in this book thinks that peanut butter tastes better than peanuts. Do your youngsters agree? Invite them to perform a taste test; then graph the results to find out which peanut treat is tops with your class.

Prepare the graph by cutting a jar shape and a peanut shape from bulletin-board paper. Label the jar cutout "Peanut Butter" and the peanut cutout "Peanuts." Mount each cutout on a wall or bulletin board. Print "Which Tastes Better?" on a sentence strip and add this title to the display.

To conduct the taste test, give each child two small paper cups—one containing a few shelled, roasted peanuts and one containing a plastic spoon with a dab of peanut butter. Have each child taste the contents of each of her cups. Then give her an index card. Ask her to write her name on her card. Have her affix her card (using Sticky-Tac) to the jar cutout or the peanut cutout to indicate her preference. As a class, count the cards on each cutout to determine which food was the class favorite.

Peanuts: Trudy, Jamal, Emil, Devin, Tanner, Amy, Eva

Peanut Butter

Josh	Miranda
April	Sam
Raul	Ben
Kate	Alex

SHALL WE SHELL?

Invite youngsters to participate in some peanut-butter preparation that will provide both math and fine-motor practice. Have the children wash their hands thoroughly before beginning. Then give each child a three-ounce paper cup filled with unshelled, roasted peanuts. Ask each child to estimate how many unshelled peanuts are in his cup. Jot his guess on a sticky note and attach the note to his cup. Then invite each child to empty the peanuts onto a tabletop and count them. Encourage him to compare his guess with the actual results.

Then show the children how to shell the peanuts. If students have difficulty breaking the peanut shells open with their hands, provide small wooden blocks for them to use as mallets. Emphasize that the children must NOT use their mouths to break open the peanuts. Invite the children to do more estimating as they break open each peanut shell. How many peanuts do they think they'll find inside each shell? Do they think all the shells hold the same number of peanuts? Provide two large bowls—one for the peanuts and one for the shells—and let the fun begin!

LET'S MAKE PEANUT BUTTER!

Once you have a cup or two of shelled peanuts, you're ready to make peanut butter in the classroom. Youngsters will be fascinated as they watch the crunchy peanuts being transformed into a creamy spread.

Pour one to two cups of shelled, roasted peanuts into a blender or food processor and process them until finely chopped. Add one tablespoon of peanut or canola oil. Blend on high until the mixture is fairly smooth. (It will not reach the same consistency as commercial peanut butter.) Stop occasionally to scrape down the bowl and show the children the progress of the peanut butter. When the mixture reaches the desired consistency, serve each child a sample of the peanut butter on a cracker. Ask them if homemade peanut butter tastes like peanut butter from the store. Provide small cups of milk or water to wash down this sticky treat. Then encourage the children to sing the popular peanut-butter tunes on this page.

A Peanut Sat On A Railroad Track
A peanut sat on a railroad track.
Its heart was all a-flutter.
A choo-choo train came 'round the bend,
Toot, toot—peanut butter!

Peanut, Peanut Butter
Chorus:
Peanut, peanut butter—jelly.
Peanut, peanut butter—jelly.

Verses:
First you take the peanuts and you smash 'em, you smash 'em.
You smash 'em, smash 'em, smash 'em. (Press palms together.)

Repeat chorus.

Continue with other verses:
Then you take a knife and you spread it… (Imitate spreading.)
Then you take the grapes and you squish 'em… (Imitate stomping grapes.)
Then you take the jelly and you spread it… (Imitate spreading.)
Then you put the bread together and you cut it… (Make a sawing motion.)
Then you bite the sandwich and you chew it… (Imitate biting a sandwich.)

Gulp! Mmmmm! (Rub tummy.)

PEANUT-BUTTER PLAY DOUGH

Have little ones help mix up a batch of peanut-butter play dough for a sensory experience that's finger-lickin' good! Combine a medium-sized jar of peanut butter with one-fourth cup of honey. Add nonfat dry milk until the mixture has the consistency of play dough. Give each child a small amount of the play dough on a sheet of waxed paper. Invite him to mold the play dough or to flatten it and use small cookie cutters to cut shapes from it. Your young sculptors can nibble as they create!

SQUISHY DIP

How about another tactile treat that's neat to eat? Pair peanut butter with its famous friend—jelly—to make "Squishy Dip." In advance, cut several apples into wedges. For each child, place three tablespoons of peanut butter and two tablespoons of jelly into a zippered sandwich bag. Seal the bag and tape the edge with masking tape to prevent leakage. Then encourage each youngster to squish the bag between his fingers. Ask youngsters to describe the feeling and appearance of the gooey mixture as the peanut butter and jelly mix together. Ask questions such as "Are the colors in your bag changing? Does the mixture feel wet? Dry? Sticky? Does it feel thick or thin?" If desired, have children "draw" on the bags with their fingers.

To complete the sensory experience, assist the children in opening their bags. Invite them to dip apple wedges into the Squishy Dip, then taste the mixture. Elicit more descriptive words as the children talk about the mixture's smell and taste.

THE STORY OF A SANDWICH

Almost everyone likes to eat peanut-butter-and-jelly sandwiches, but some folks like to pair peanut butter with not-so-traditional sandwich fixings. Find out what your little ones like on their peanut-butter sandwiches when they create this class book.

For each child, duplicate the peanut-butter-on-bread pattern on page 25 on a sheet of white construction paper. Have each child cut out the slice of bread. Then have him draw a food item of his choice inside the peanut-butter outline. (Or have each child cut a picture of a food item from a magazine and glue it inside the outline.) Fill in each child's dictation at the bottom of his page. Then invite him to color the remaining area inside the peanut-butter outline with a brown crayon. Use one of the cut-out pages to trace two slice-of-bread shapes on white construction paper. Cut these out to use as front and back covers for the book. On one, print the title "The Perfect Peanut-Butter Sandwich." Stack the finished pages between the covers and staple along the left edge. Then share this tantalizing tale with your sandwich chefs during group time.

The Perfect Peanut-Butter Sandwich

Jackson

likes

banana

on a peanut-butter sandwich.

23

PARTIAL TO PEANUT BUTTER?

If so, then you'll love these fun and easy recipes! Try one or more of them with your young peanut-butter buffs in celebration of Peanut Butter Lovers' Month.

Peanutty Sandwich Shapes

• peanut butter thinned with a small amount of corn syrup
• one slice of bread per child
• a variety of toppings, such as pretzel sticks, raisins, sunflower seeds, grape halves, and shredded cheese

Invite each child to use a plastic knife or a craft stick to spread some peanut butter on a slice of bread. Have him use a cookie cutter to cut a shape from the bread. Encourage him to decorate his cutout with the toppings of his choice.

Frosty Peanut-Butter Squares

• 1/2 cup packed brown sugar
• 3/4 cup corn syrup
• 3/4 cup peanut butter
• 1/3 cup raisins
• 6–7 cups frosted cornflakes

In an electric skillet, heat the sugar, corn syrup, and peanut butter over low heat. Stir until the mixture is soft and well blended. Add the raisins and cereal, and blend well. Spoon the mixture into a buttered, 8-inch square pan and cool. Cut into 16 squares and serve.

Salty S'mores

• peanut butter
• one saltine cracker per child
• one marshmallow per child

Have each child use a plastic knife or a craft stick to spread some peanut butter on a saltine cracker. Have him place a marshmallow on top of the peanut butter. Place the s'more under the broiler in a toaster oven until the marshmallow is a light golden brown. Cool slightly and serve.

Peanut-Butter Pizza

• peanut butter thinned with a small amount of corn syrup
• one English-muffin half per child
• a variety of toppings, such as banana wheels, miniature marshmallows, raisins, or cake sprinkles
• honey in a squeeze bottle (optional)

Have each child use a plastic knife or a craft stick to spread peanut butter on an English-muffin half. Encourage him to add the toppings of his choice to his pizza. If desired, have each child drizzle a small amount of honey over his pizza before eating it.

_____

likes

_____

on a peanut-butter sandwich.

Note to the Teacher: Use with "The Story Of A Sandwich" on page 23.

25

SAFETY SENSE

Since most youngsters are already familiar with their five senses, encourage their awareness of a different kind of sense—safety sense—at school.

ideas contributed by Mackie Rhodes and Amy Zierow

To Eat Or Not To Eat

Youngsters will enjoy digesting this safety surprise while they learn to distinguish between edible and nonedible items in the classroom. Purchase several individually sized packages of a variety of snacks, such as M&M's®, popcorn, peanuts, pretzels, raisins, and corn chips. Create packages of nonfood items by placing sets of snap-together blocks, small plastic counters, buttons, glue sticks, and other similar items in separate resealable plastic sandwich bags. Place each of the food and nonfood packages into a large paper bag. Invite a child to reach into the bag and remove one package. Have him decide whether the package contains things that *can* or *cannot* be eaten. If the package contains edible items, have the child open and empty that bag into a large bowl. If the package contains nonfood items, have the child place that bag in a box. Ask students to explain why they shouldn't put these items in their mouths. In turn, invite other volunteers to remove packages from the paper bag until it is empty. After all the food packages have been poured into the bowl, stir the mixture; then serve each child a portion of this tasty safety surprise on a small paper plate.

Busy Pairs Of Hands

Recite this handy rhyme to remind youngsters of appropriate ways to use their hands safely at school. Duplicate page 34 for later use; then mount page 33 on tagboard. Cut out each pair of hands and laminate them for durability. Attach the hook side of a piece of self-adhesive Velcro® to the back of each pair of hands. To use, place the hands on a flannelboard. While reciting this rhyme, have a volunteer remove one pair of hands for each verse. Encourage all the children to hold their hands in front of them during the last verse, then point to "you" and "me" as the rhyme is completed.

Five pairs of hands as busy as can be.
All work and play so carefully.

Four pairs of hands safe from pinches and sores,
Don't use broken toys or slam doors and drawers.

Three pairs of hands, in the sand they go,
Play oh so nicely—they do not throw.

Two pairs of hands use scissors with care,
And cut what they should—not clothes; not hair.

One pair of hands stays far away
From outlets and plugs—they're not for play.

Each pair of hands as good as can be
Keeps school safe and sound for you and me.

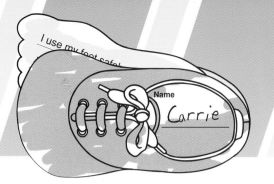

Safety In A Shoe

Encourage each student to put his best foot forward with this message-in-a-shoe idea. For each child, copy the foot and shoe patterns on page 32 on white construction paper. Cut out each of the patterns; then cut one additional construction-paper outline of the shoe pattern for each child. Explain to students that their feet enable them to do lots of fun things such as climb playground equipment and kick a ball. Encourage students to brainstorm appropriate ways they can use their feet at school. Write their suggestions on a sheet of chart paper. Then have them discuss some unsafe uses of their feet, such as kicking others and climbing furniture. Ask each child to write his name on the shoe pattern and to write or dictate an ending to the sentence on the foot pattern, "I use my feet safely when _____." Have him color the foot and shoe patterns. To make a shoe, help each student glue the shoe pattern to the shoe outline along the edges of the shoe, leaving the inner shoe edge open. When the glue dries, slip the foot cutout into the opening of the shoe. Encourage youngsters to share their feet safety messages with one another.

Tell When You Need Help

Youngsters will show that they got the safety message when they illustrate safe ways to handle difficult situations at school. Have students discuss ways that they can get their needs met or resolve conflicts. Find out how they would respond in these, or similar, situations:

- A child needs to get an item from a high shelf.
- A child sees a classmate fall off a swing.
- A child has a disagreement with a classmate.

As each situation is discussed, help students understand that problems can be resolved by talking about them or asking for help. Emphasize that the safe way to handle many situations is to tell an adult. Afterwards, have each child illustrate a situation on a sheet of white construction paper programmed with "I tell someone when I _____." Encourage him to dictate an ending to the sentence. Display the pictures on a bulletin board decorated with a large construction-paper mouth and the title "Tell When You Need Help!"

Safety Simon Says

Encourage little ones to listen to and follow directions with this safety version of the Simon Says game. Explain to students that they will be given many directions, but they should only follow the safe directions—those that "Safety Simon" says they should follow. Then present directions at random, giving some to represent safe actions such as "Walk quietly" and "Put your hands by your sides," and others to represent unsafe actions such as "Slide across the room," and "Climb onto the table." Begin each safe movement or direction with the phrase "Safety Simon says..." For each unsafe direction, be prepared to quickly remind students that Safety Simon did not say to do that one so they should not respond to it. To conclude the game, have Safety Simon direct the children in giving themselves a big safety squeeze (hug) for being good listeners and following directions so well.

27

One at a time

Safe Play Is The Best Way!

Give little ones the opportunity to express their understanding of safe playground behaviors with these safety posters. In advance, draw simple pictures of the various pieces of playground equipment at your school on half-sheets of poster board. The posters may show items such as a slide, swing set, seesaw, climbing structure, tricycle, wagon, or any other piece of equipment that you want to use to emphasize safety. Prepare a tray of tempera paint and a person-shaped sponge. Explain to youngsters that the playground equipment is available for their enjoyment; however, it must be used safely. Show the students one of the posters, and have them discuss the safe way to use that piece of equipment. For instance, for the slide poster, emphasize that while one student sits at the top of the slide, one should stand on the ladder to wait his turn, and another should wait in line at the bottom of the ladder. Then ask a volunteer to dip the sponge in the paint and stamp a person outline at each safe place on the picture of the slide. Write a student-dictated phrase about a safe way to use that piece of equipment at the bottom of the poster. For example, a student may dictate "One at a time" as a safe way to play on the slide. Follow the same procedure for each of the other posters. Display the completed posters near the door with the title "Safe Play Is The Best Way!" Periodically call the students' attention to the posters as they prepare to go outdoors to play.

Safe Or Not?

Promote listening and thinking skills with these puppets that help emphasize the importance of playground safety. Duplicate the puppet pattern on page 34 for each child. Have each child color both sections of the puppet. Help him cut the pattern along the bold line; then fold the puppet in half. Insert the end of a craft stick between the two sides of the folded paper; secure the craft stick and the open edges of the paper with tape. Explain to youngsters that the happy face on their puppets represents a safe way to play—"Okay!"—while the sad face represents an unsafe way to play—"Oops!" After sharing a made-up description of a playground situation, or one from the provided list, have each student show the side of his puppet that indicates whether a safe or unsafe playground situation was described. Encourage each student to say "Okay!" or "Oops!" to correspond to the side of the puppet he displays. Then encourage students to discuss each situation, telling the safe ways to respond in the unsafe situations.

- Rowena is swinging. Jennifer runs in front of the swing to catch a ball.
- John sits on the slide right behind Robert.
- Tommy waits at the bottom of the ladder until Sarah sits on the slide to take her turn.
- Amber jumps out of the wagon while it is moving.
- Jay and Courtney take turns crawling through the tunnel.
- Shondra rides her tricycle carefully around her friends.
- Joshua and Malcolm sit on the same side of the seesaw.
- Kylie and Ivan climb the fence to get the ball on the other side.
- Leeron stops the wagon so that Orin can get on it.

Take It Or Leave It

Use this activity to help students think about whether those tempting objects of curiosity found on the ground should be picked up or left alone. To prepare, cut a long strip of brown butcher paper to represent the ground. Collect a number of items that children should leave alone while playing outside, such as a rock, stick, nail, pinecone, used Band-Aid®, and broken glass. Also gather items that may be found outside, but are safe for children to pick up, such as a sheet of paper, coin, bookbag, jacket, ball, and pen. Spread the butcher paper out on the floor; then randomly place the items on the paper. In turn invite volunteers to select and remove an item that is safe to pick up off the playground. When all the safe items have been removed, have students discuss why the remaining items are unsafe to pick up or touch. Explain that some of the leftover items are not dangerous unless they are used in an unsafe way. For example, rocks and sticks are not harmful, but can become dangerous if they are thrown. Request that children who enjoy playing safely with natural items, such as drawing in the dirt with sticks or building structures with stones, seek permission before using these things on the playground.

Safety On The Playground

Take students on a trip to the playground for the opportunity to show off their knowledge of playground safety. In advance, duplicate a copy of the certificate on page 34 for each child. If possible, arrange for several volunteers or older students to help with the supervision of children in this activity. Divide your class into groups of four or five children. Assign a supervisor and a piece of playground equipment to each group. Have the students in each group tell about, then demonstrate, the safe and appropriate ways to use their assigned playground equipment. After each child has had a turn on his assigned equipment, rotate the groups to another piece of equipment so that each child has the opportunity to play safely on all the available equipment. Then invite the students to freely choose to play on any of the equipment on the playground. Observe and praise them for playing safely. When necessary, remind students of the safe way to play.

I'm in the **swing** of playground safety!

Name: Brooke

Ask me to tell you about the safe ways I play.

Afterwards, present each child with a personalized copy of the certificate for safe play on the playground. Encourage students to take their certificates home to share with their families.

Stay Together

With the help of this follow-the-leader activity, youngsters who are ready to begin walking in a line will be able to practice staying safely together whenever the class walks down the hall or outdoors. To begin, explain to students that walking in a line can contribute to their safety at school. When students are in a line, the teacher is able to more easily see each person. Walking in a line also keeps the hallways passable for other groups of children. During fire drills and other emergencies, children can be moved more quickly and safely while in a line. To demonstrate what a line is, place a long strip of masking tape in a straight line along the floor. Have students stand one behind the other on the tape to form a line. Then have each child place his hands on the shoulders of the child in front of him. In follow-the-leader fashion, encourage the first child in line to lead the others in a walk down the hall and back again to the room. After returning to the room, invite a different child to be the line leader. Have students line up again to repeat the activity, instructing the leader to walk to a different location. Following a few rounds of walking in line as described, have the students walk in line several more times with their hands at their sides. Remind each child to watch and follow the child in front of her. Provide opportunities for students to walk in a line for long distances through hallways, on sidewalks, and on stairs. To further reinforce the concept of a line, draw a straight line on a sheet of paper programmed with "We stay together in a line." Duplicate the page for each child. Provide her with people and animal stickers to place along the line on the paper.

We stay together in a line.

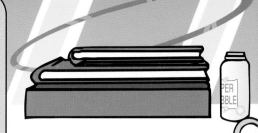

The Buddy Bubble

Promote responsibility and independence in youngsters with the use of a "buddy bubble." In advance, prepare short errands for students to perform. For example, place a different shape outside the doors of several nearby rooms for students to retrieve, or have a box of books or toys to be taken to a different area of the room. To help little ones understand the concept of the buddy system, divide the class into pairs, explaining that each child's partner is his buddy. Then have a pair of students hold a large Hula-Hoop® around themselves. Tell the children that the hoop represents a "buddy bubble" and that they are to stay together inside the bubble as they run their errand. Give the pair their assignment; then encourage them to stay together as they complete it. When their assignment is completed, invite the students to burst their buddy bubble by stepping out of the Hula-Hoop®. Give each pair of students the opportunity to perform an assignment using the buddy bubble. Emphasize that when the children are sent on an errand with a buddy, it is for their safety that they remain together the entire time. Afterwards, offer the student partners a bottle of bubble solution to share during playtime.

Stay in seats.

Removable GLU-STIK

A Safe Ride

If you have students who ride a school bus or van, use this song to emphasize safety rules for riding. Prior to singing the song, write each bus safety rule from the song on a separate sheet of bus-shaped notepaper. Attach each notepaper to a sheet of chart paper using a removable adhesive glue stick. Invite a volunteer to remove one of the bus notes. Read the rule to the class, then sing that rule in the song. For those children who ride in a car, adapt the song by replacing the words "on the bus" with "in the car."

The Children On The Bus
(sung to the tune of "The Wheels On The Bus")

The children on the bus
[stay in their seats, in their seats, in their seats,]
The children on the bus [stay in their seats]
On the way to school.

Repeat the song, replacing the underlined words with *talk quietly, keep hands inside, listen to adults,* or *ride carefully.*

Safety Search

Accompany youngsters on a safety walk to search for the many safe features around your school. During the walk, encourage children to point out and tell about the things that make their school safe. Help them identify items inside the building, such as fire extinguishers and alarms, sprinkler systems, and exit signs. Outdoors, guide students to note the sidewalks, crosswalks, vehicle signs, and speed bumps around the school. After the safety walk, encourage students to recall the safety items they observed. Write the names of the items on a sheet of chart paper. Ask the children to tell how each item makes your school safe.

Bus Safety

Little ones will enjoy making these books to demonstrate their knowledge of bus safety. In advance, duplicate a class quantity of the book cover pattern on page 35 on yellow construction paper. Cut out each bus pattern; then trace the pattern on a sheet of yellow construction paper for each child. Cut out the bus outline to be used as the back cover of the book. For the pages of each book, cut several white construction-paper bus outlines for each child.

Engage those students who ride a bus to school in a discussion about appropriate ways to wait for the bus, such as staying on the sidewalk and avoiding overly active play. Then encourage all students to discuss appropriate ways to get on and off the bus, such as waiting in line for their turn to get on and remaining seated until the bus stops. If possible, invite the children to practice some of these safety guidelines using a real bus or van. (Or set up an imaginary bus in the classroom to use for practice.) Then give each child a few sheets of the white bus cutouts. On each page, have her illustrate a safe way to behave on or around a bus. Encourage her to write or dictate a sentence to describe each illustration. Place the completed pages between the yellow bus covers; then staple them together along the top edge. Have the child write her name in the space provided. Encourage each youngster to share her book with a partner.

31

Foot Pattern

Use with "Safety In A Shoe" on page 27.

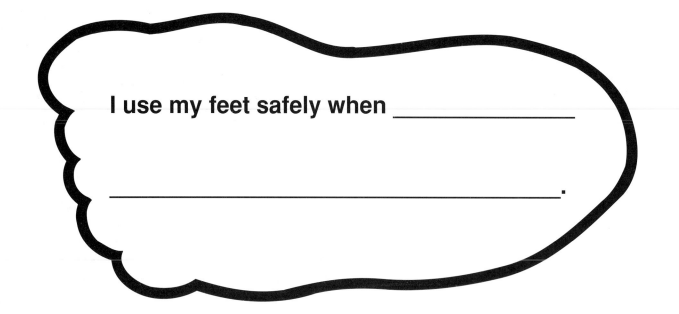

I use my feet safely when _____

_____.

Shoe Pattern

Use with "Safety In A Shoe" on page 27.

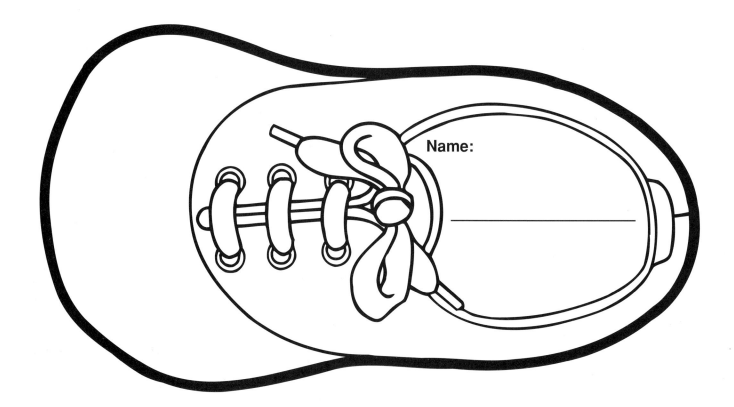

Name:

_____

Puppet Pattern
Use with "Safe Or Not?" on page 28.

Certificate
Use with "Safety On The Playground" on page 29.

I'm in the

swing

of playground safety!

Name:

_____

Ask me to tell you about the safe ways I play.

BUS SAFETY

By _____

BIG IDEAS FOR BOOK WEEK

Celebrate National Children's Book Week—the third week in November—with this collection of activities designed to capture the interest of your little bookworms.
ideas contributed by Valerie SchifferDanoff and Ada Hanley Goren

Ten Clever Classroom Reading Centers

Consider setting up an unusual reading center in your classroom. The extra effort will be worth it when you see the excitement generated as little ones visit the center to read and share books. Choose a center that will be appealing and provide a safe setting for the age level of your youngsters.

1. **"Read, Read, Read A Book"**—Bring in an old rowboat or canoe. Set it on top of a large blue sheet or shower curtain to simulate water. Fill the boat with fluffy pillows and books; then encourage youngsters to float away into the land of imagination.
2. **"Dive Into Books"**—Fill an inflatable kiddie pool with comfy pillows and inflatable swim rings or pool toys. Invite students to jump in and splash around with a good book!
3. **"Reading In Bed"**—Set up bunk beds, complete with pillows and "snuggly" blankets. Be sure to add some flashlights for reading under the covers!
4. **"Camp Out With A Good Book"**—Set up a tent with sleeping bags and a battery-operated lamp. Invite students to crawl inside and enjoy a backpack full of books.
5. **"Come Read With Me Down By The Sea"**—Set out some beach chairs, beach towels, and coolers filled with books. Add a bright lamp and a few pairs of child-sized sunglasses. Ahhh...there's nothing like a good book at the beach!
6. **"The Garden Of Reading"**—Surround a simple wooden bench with potted plants and hanging baskets. Have students "pick" books from large flowerpots and baskets. Children's appreciation for reading will be in full bloom!
7. **" 'Bear-y' Good Readers"**—Set up a few beanbag chairs and a large assortment of teddy bears. Encourage children to read to and with their furry friends.
8. **"Books In The Bathtub"**—Cut off one long side of an appliance box to create a bathtub. Paint the box white and partially fill it with Styrofoam® packing pieces. Add a vinyl tub pillow and a rubber ducky to complete the effect. Rub-a-dub-dub! Let's read books in the tub!
9. **"Relax And Read"**—Set up a freestanding canvas hammock and a few pillows to entice little ones to lie back and enjoy a good story.
10. **"Pack A Picnic Basket With Books"**—Bring in a child-sized picnic table or a checkered tablecloth to spread on the floor. Add a few picnic baskets full of good books, and let the reading feast begin!

Get Ready, Get Set,...

During Book Week, you'll want to immerse your youngsters in books. So prepare by filling your classroom with a wide variety of books. Check out books from your school and public libraries, and put them *everywhere*—in your reading area, on your chalkboard ledge, in baskets, on tables, and in each of your centers. Include both fiction and nonfiction selections to appeal to the tastes of each of your students.

Then create a bookworm puppet to guide your class through their Book Week activities. Obtain a long, green sock and a pair of wiggle eyes. Fashion a pair of glasses for your puppet from a pipe cleaner. Hot-glue the wiggle eyes and glasses securely to the toe end of the sock. Slip the sock over one hand, and Buddy the Bookworm is ready to go!

A Bookworm's Booklet

National Children's Book Week is a good time to teach children how to care for books. Use your Buddy-the-Bookworm puppet to lead this discussion. Remind students of some basic rules for handling books, such as:

- Do not draw on books.
- Do not cut or tear a book's pages or covers.
- Turn the pages of a book carefully.
- Put books away when you are finished.

Then have little ones create fun reproducible booklets to help them remember some proper ways to care for books. Duplicate a copy of page 42 for each child. Have each youngster cut the booklet cover and pages apart on the bold lines, then color each of the illustrations. Assist each child in stacking the pages in the correct order and stapling them together along the left side. Then have each child use a hole puncher (making multiple punches) to create a hole, as indicated, through all four thicknesses of paper.

Before reading through the booklet, use a fine-tipped marker to draw a face on the tip of each child's right index finger. Have him insert his finger through the holes in his booklet. Now his personal bookworm is ready to read the booklet! Encourage little ones to share their booklets with family members at home.

I Am A Bookworm
by
Charles

Through The Looking Glasses

Youngsters will delight in wearing these very special glasses, designed to help them learn more about books. For each child, duplicate the glasses pattern on page 44 on white construction paper or tagboard. Encourage each child to color her pattern and cut it out on the bold lines. Then assist each child in cutting out the eyeholes and stapling a pipe-cleaner earpiece to each side of her glasses. (Place a small piece of masking tape over each staple and pipe-cleaner end to avoid scratching.) Bend the end of each pipe cleaner to fit around the child's ears. Then invite each child to don her glasses and recite the poem, "Look Through A Book."

Look Through A Book

I look through a book,
And what do I see?
I see words
Written so carefully.

I look through a book,
And what do I see?
I see pictures
Pretty as can be.

I look through a book,
And what do I see?
I see adventures
For you and for me!

Invite the children to wear their glasses again for the activity described in "Let's Take A Book Walk."

Let's Take A Book Walk

Use your Buddy-the-Bookworm puppet to explain to students that the special glasses made in "Through The Looking Glasses" will help them look at all the parts of a book. Hold up a picture book. Guide the students to identify and discuss the basic parts of the book—including the cover, title, author's name, illustrator's name, title page, dedication, and page numbers. Read through the book one time. Then go back and reread each page, pointing out the text and noting which parts of the story are illustrated.

At another group time, have the children put on their special glasses again. Read through a book, covering the illustrations with a sheet of construction paper. Have the children imagine and describe what the pictures might look like. Then reread the book, showing the illustrations to the children. Choose another book. Cover the words and ask the children to make up a story to match the pictures. Then read the book's actual text. Have the children compare the author's story to their version.

Interview The Author

Periodically throughout National Children's Book Week, focus students' attention on the authors and illustrators of their favorite stories. Read some biographical information and share photos of authors from book jackets. If possible, invite a local author to visit the class to talk about her work. Then encourage your youngsters to become authors. Set aside time each day for children to "write" stories. Share a wordless book and reassure students that stories can be told through pictures alone.

Then give each youngster a turn to share the spotlight as Today's Author. Make this a special event by designating a special author's chair with the sign on page 43. First duplicate page 44 for later use. Then cut around the border of the sign on page 43 and glue the sign to a sheet of tagboard. Laminate the sign for durability. Attach it to the back of a child-sized chair. Tie a bunch of balloons to the chair for an extra special touch. On each child's turn, invite him to sit in the chair as he shares one of his stories. Then give the author's classmates a chance to interview him about his story and himself. Encourage children to ask the author questions about his home, his family, his interests, and his story. Continue your Today's Author feature beyond your Book Week festivities, so that each child has several turns to share his stories throughout the year.

A Bookworm Bookmark

Invite each child to create a bookmark with a likeness of her pal, Buddy the Bookworm! Give each child a 2" x 5" strip of tagboard, a four-inch length of wide green ribbon, a crayon, scissors, glue, and two wiggle eyes. First, have each child write her name on one side of her tagboard strip. Then invite each child to trim the ends of her ribbon to resemble the shape of a fat, wriggly worm. Have her glue the ribbon to the blank side of the tagboard strip, then glue the two wiggle eyes near one end of the ribbon. Allow the glue to dry thoroughly before using the bookmarks.

The Family Connection

Invite family members to visit your classroom as guest readers during your Book Week festivities. Duplicate a copy of the parent letter on page 45 for each child to take home. If a parent can't come in person, she may be able to make a cassette recording of herself reading a favorite story. After receiving parents' responses, schedule visits from your guest readers and send home blank cassette tapes to those parents who volunteered to make recordings.

The parent letter also describes the activities in "The Book-Borrowing Bag" on this page and "Book Exchange" on page 41.

The Book-Borrowing Bag

Create a colorful, canvas tote bag that will help little ones safely transport classroom books between school and home. Purchase a medium-sized canvas tote bag with sturdy handles. Use fabric paints to create a cute bookworm design on one side of the bag. Then use a laundry marker to write your name, room number, and school name. Each day, encourage one child to choose a book from your classroom library to borrow. Place the book in the Book-Borrowing Bag and have the child take it home to share with family members. When he returns the book and bag on the next school day, another child may have a turn to borrow a book.

Where The Books Are

All this talk about books should have your youngsters hungry for more, more, more! Plan a field trip to the public library or a local bookstore. Prior to your visit, arrange for a librarian or bookstore employee to guide the students on a tour of the facility. During the tour, give children a chance to browse through the shelves of books. Provide them with information about proper behavior and procedures while in the library or store. If the tour includes a storytime, encourage students to sit quietly and listen carefully to the story. At the conclusion of the tour, have the class decide on a few books to check out from the library or purchase from the bookstore for your classroom.

After your field trip, encourage the children to role-play what they've experienced. Transform your dramatic play area into a library or bookstore for a week or two. Add a shelf of books and magazines and some other simple props, such as index cards (for library cards), a date stamp, or a toy cash register. Encourage youngsters to take turns role-playing the library or bookstore workers and the patrons.

A Book Week Bash

Culminate your Book Week unit with a classroom celebration. Invite parents to join you for a storybook parade, a festive book exchange, and some yummy Book Week bites!

Book Exchange

What's a party without presents? Invite each family (by way of the parent letter on page 45) to donate a book for the book exchange. Wrap a few extra books in case you don't receive enough donations. Place each child's festively wrapped book in a large basket or box. During the party, have each youngster choose a book to unwrap and take home. Or ask the children to donate their books to the class library, so that everyone can enjoy them.

A Storybook Parade

Little ones love to participate in parades! Encourage each child to show off his favorite book in a special Book Week promenade. Use a large, zippered plastic bag and a 30-inch length of yarn to make a storybook necklace for each child. Punch a hole in each side of the bag, just below the zippered closure. Thread each end of the yarn through a hole and tie it securely. Invite each child to place his favorite paperback book into the zippered bag, then slip the necklace over his head so that the book's cover faces outward as the bag rests on his chest. Then have youngsters line up and parade through your school, showing off their book choices to the other students, teachers, and parent visitors.

Bite A Book

Once you're back in the classroom, conclude the festivities with a special snack. Have the children create book-shaped snacks with cover illustrations of their favorite bookworm—Buddy! Give each child two graham-cracker squares (to serve as the book's front and back covers). Invite her to use a plastic knife to spread canned white frosting (to represent the book's white pages) on one cracker, then top it with the other cracker. Then have her squeeze a thick line of green decorator tube icing onto the book's cover to create a likeness of Buddy the Bookworm. To make Buddy's glasses, have her place two pieces of Cheerios® cereal and two short pieces of a pretzel stick at the top end of her green icing worm, as shown. Then invite each child to bite into a good book—her Book Week snack!

41

Booklet Cover And Pages

Use with "A Bookworm's Booklet" on page 37.

I treat books gently.

2

I Am A Bookworm

by

I put books away.

3

I keep books clean.

1

Glasses Pattern
Use with "Through The Looking Glasses" and "Let's Take A Book Walk" on page 38.

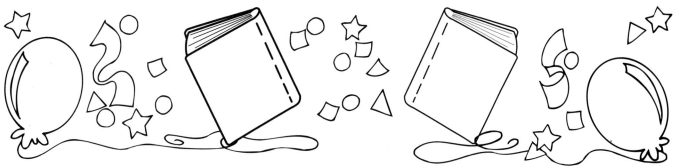

Dear Family,

We will be celebrating National Children's Book Week during the week of November _____. We have planned some very special activities, and we'd like to invite you to participate in one or more of the following ways:

_____ Would you like to be a guest reader in our classroom? Please indicate if you can join us to read a story aloud to the children.

_____ If you are unable to visit us in person, would you like to make a cassette recording of one of your child's favorite stories? We'd love to hear your voice in our listening center! Please indicate your interest, so I can send you a blank cassette tape.

_____ Could you send in a book for our book exchange? Please choose a book your child is willing to donate. Wrap it in gift paper and ribbon, and send it to school on _____. (date) Each child will have the opportunity to choose a book donated by a classmate.

Also, each child will be bringing home our Book-Borrowing Bag with a book from our classroom library. Please share the book with your child and return it in the bag on the next school day. Enjoy reading with your child!

Please return this form by _____ to indicate your participation. (date)

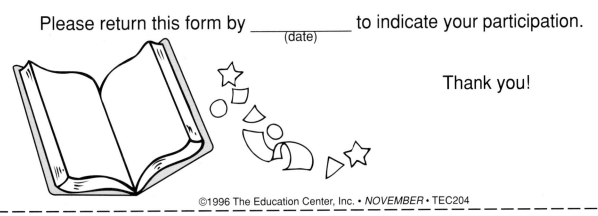

Thank you!

Note To The Teacher: Use this with "The Family Connection" and "The Book Borrowing Bag" on page 40 and "Book Exchange" on page 41.

All Systems Are Go....

...for exciting activities centered around outer space! Invite each of your youngsters to earn the title of Space Ace as he explores concepts and skills associated with space and astronauts. It'll be a blast!

by Ada Hanley Goren

Astronaut Adventures

Begin your study by reading aloud *I Want To Be An Astronaut* by Byron Barton (HarperCollins Publishers). Discuss the vocabulary words that may be unfamiliar to young children, such as *zero gravity, satellite,* and *orbit.* Then ask students to tell what they already know about astronauts and space travel. After hearing the children's ideas, share a photo-illustrated book, such as *If You Were An Astronaut* by Dinah L. Moché (Western Publishing Company, Inc.). You may want to paraphrase some of the text to suit your students' understanding. Point out that astronauts must go through extensive training to learn about space and to prepare for travel away from Earth. Then pose the question, "Would *you* like to be an astronaut?" You're sure to get some enthusiastic responses!

Getting Ready

Tell youngsters that—even though they're too young to train to become real astronauts—you'd like to invite them to become Space Aces. Show the children one of the "Space Ace In Training" badges you have prepared (see below). Explain that, as each child completes each activity in your space unit, she will receive a star sticker on her badge. At the end of the unit, she will have earned the title "Space Ace" and will be ready for some imaginary space travel!

Prepare for your Space Ace training by purchasing a large supply of foil star stickers. Duplicate a class supply of the badge pattern on page 55 on tagboard or white construction paper. Have each child color and cut out her badge. Use your preferred method to attach the badge to her shirt— rolled masking tape or a safety pin. Each day during your space unit, have each child wear her badge. As she completes each activity with a numbered star, affix a star sticker to her "Space Ace In Training" badge.

Engineers At Work

Begin your Space Ace training with some creative engineering. Invite youngsters to help you design and build a shuttle for their imaginary space travels. In advance obtain a large appliance box. Cut out a door and porthole using a utility knife. Then collect a variety of items such as small gift boxes, cardboard tubes, disposable plastic containers, and jug lids. Gather some photos of real space shuttles and rockets to provide youngsters with inspiration. Lithographs are available from the NASA Teacher Resource Center that serves your state. (You can get the address and phone number for your state's center by calling [216] 774-1051, Ext. 293 or 294, or writing NASA CORE, Lorain County Joint Vocational School, 15181 Rt. 58 South, Oberlin, OH 44074.)

Working with one small group at a time, have the students help you design and construct the shuttle craft. Have each group help with a different stage of construction—such as painting the craft or gluing on the gathered items to simulate booster rockets, wings, lights, or handles. Encourage one group to design and build a control panel on the inside of the craft, as well. When the shuttle is finished, invite small groups of youngsters to visit it periodically throughout your space unit. Then keep it in your dramatic play area for a few weeks for your Space Aces to enjoy.

Sample Some Space Food

In preparation for their travels, give your trainees a little taste of life as an astronaut. Explain to little ones that astronauts eat specially prepared foods when they are traveling in space. The astronauts' food must be lightweight, must take up very little storage space, and must need no refrigeration. Introduce the word *dehydrated.* Tell students that dehydrated foods have had the water or juices removed from them (making them weigh less). Provide some dried foods—such as apple or banana chips, beef jerky, raisins, or fruit rolls—for students to sample. If desired, purchase an example of freeze-dried food for students to taste. Pouches of freeze-dried foods can be purchased at science and nature shops and museums. (Call Action Products International, Inc., at 1-800-772-2846 to find out the name of the store nearest you.) How about an astronaut version of cheese pizza or strawberry ice cream for snacktime today?

Astronaut Exercises

Astronauts must be in top physical condition to endure the rigors of space travel. Get your Space Ace trainees in shape with an out-of-this-world workout!

Solar System Stretch—Reach to the sky; then stretch arms out wide.
Rocket Ship Run-In-Place—Warm up and get ready to take off!
Galactic Gallop—Gallop all around the galaxy (your classroom).
Lunar Leaps—Jump as far as you can.
Trainee Toe-Touches—Touch your toes ten times.
Planet Push-ups—Do nine push-ups—one for each planet!
Constellation Cooldown—Lie down on your back. Relax as you imagine staring up at a starry sky.

Bodies In Space

Now it's time for your trainees to learn about the objects in outer space. Ask youngsters, "Where are the moon and the sun?" Children will most likely answer that these objects are in the sky. Explain that the moon and sun are indeed in the sky—the space surrounding the Earth. Then have youngsters role-play the relationship of the Earth, its moon, and the sun as follows: Ask one child to play the part of the sun and stand in front of the group. Using chalk or masking tape, make a large circle on the floor around the child. Ask another child to play the part of Earth. Have him walk on the line around the sun. Tell students that this is how the Earth moves in an *orbit,* or circle, around the sun. Have the child portraying Earth stop on the chalk line. Have him hold a Hula-Hoop® around his middle. Then ask a third child to role-play the moon. Have him stand beside the Hula-Hoop® and follow its line in an orbit around Earth. Explain that this is how the moon moves around the Earth. Challenge your actors to role-play both the moon's and the Earth's orbits simultaneously. Repeat this activity until each child has had a turn to play one of the parts.

 # The Moon

Your little ones will be aglow with knowledge about Earth's closest neighbor—the moon—when you share these facts with them:
- There is no air or water on the moon.
- Because there is no air to carry sounds, it is very quiet on the moon.
- Because there is no water on the moon, its surface is very dusty and dry.
- The ground on the moon has many *craters.* These craters were formed when big space rocks crashed into the moon and left sunken areas.
- If you visited the moon, you would be able to jump very high, because there is less *gravity* on the moon than on Earth. *Gravity* is the pulling force that keeps you from floating away and gives you weight.
- Astronauts have visited the moon and walked on it. Their footprints are still there because there is no wind or water to smooth them away.

I'm the moon.

I'm the Earth.

Creating Craters

After talking about the moon and sharing some photos of the moon from a nonfiction book, invite small groups of youngsters to create some craters in your sand table. Partially fill the table with sand and smooth the surface. Provide a variety of objects—such as marbles, tennis balls, golf balls, Ping-Pong® balls, and beads—for students to drop onto the sand. Have the students observe the indentation, or crater, each object makes. Guide their discoveries by asking questions like, "Which object made the widest crater? Which made the deepest crater? Which makes a deeper crater—a golf ball or a Ping-Pong® ball? Why?" Encourage students to talk about the differences in size and weight of each object they use.

"Where Does The Sun Go At Night?"

To answer that question, try this simple experiment using your classroom globe and school photos of two of your students. Working with one small group of students at a time, show them the location of your city or state on the globe. Tape one child's photo to that area of the globe. Ask the children to imagine that the other child has gone on a trip to the other side of the world. Tape the second child's photo to the opposite side of the globe. Set the globe on a tabletop. Ask a child to shine a flashlight on the side of the globe where your city is located. Explain that the flashlight represents the light from the sun. Ask your youngsters which pictured student has the imaginary sun shining on her. Explain that she is experiencing *daytime*. Ask the students which pictured child is not in the sunshine. Explain that he is experiencing *nighttime*. As the child continues to shine the flashlight on the globe, spin the globe around slowly so that the other photo is in the light. Repeat the questions.

Explain to children that the sun shines all the time. We cannot always see it because the Earth spins. Only part of the Earth is facing the sun at any one time. When our part of the Earth faces the sun, we experience daytime. When our part of the Earth faces away from the sun, we experience nighttime. Repeat the activity with the other groups.

If desired, follow up this activity by reading one of these sunny selections:

Sun Up, Sun Down
by Gail Gibbons
Harcourt Brace Jovanovich, Publishers

Under The Sun
by Ellen Kandoian
Dodd, Mead & Company
(This book is out of print.
Check your local library.)

The Sun—A Shining Star

Share these facts about our favorite star—the sun—to enlighten your Space Ace trainees:
- The sun is a star. It looks much bigger than the other stars because it is closer to us.
- The sun is a very hot ball of fiery gases.
- People cannot visit the sun. It is too hot and there is no ground to land on.
- We get our heat and light from the sun.
- The Earth travels around the sun in an orbit.

Twinkle, Twinkle

Stars will be familiar to all children who have gazed skyward on a dark, clear night. Introduce the topic of stars by singing "Twinkle, Twinkle, Little Star" with your students. Then tell students that stars are very similar to the sun, but are so much farther away that they appear as tiny dots of light to us here on Earth. Teach youngsters this poem to help them remember some simple information about stars.

There are so many stars, you know,
I can't even count them.
I'd like to be an astronaut
And learn some more about them.

I know stars twinkle in the sky.
I know they're far away.
I might become an astronaut
And visit them someday!
—Ada Hanley Goren

Our Planetary Neighbors

Introduce your little ones to Earth's neighbors—the *planets*. To prepare the planet cutouts on page 53, first duplicate page 54 for later use. (You may also want to make a few color copies of page 53 for later use. See the Planet Concentration game in the next paragraph.) Then glue page 53 to a sheet of tagboard, cut out the planet patterns, and laminate them if desired. Show children the cutouts and explain that each of the planets is found in our immediate space neighborhood—the *solar system.* Each planet—including Earth—revolves around the sun. More advanced students may want to learn the planets' names and see their positions around the sun. If desired, attach the hook side of a piece of self-adhesive Velcro® to the back of each planet and show students their order on a flannelboard. Even if your youngsters are too young to remember all the planet names or factual information about each one, they'll enjoy using the planet cutouts to practice skills.

Ask students to place the planet cutouts in order by size or to sort them by color or other characteristics. Or create a Planet Concentration game. Make two color copies of the planet cutouts. Cut the planets out and glue each cutout to an equal-sized tagboard square. Laminate the cards if desired. To play, mix up the cards; then spread them out facedown on a tabletop. Invite each player, in turn, to turn over two cards in an attempt to find a match.

Counting On Stars

Use star shapes to help youngsters practice sequencing the numerals one through ten. Die-cut ten star shapes from yellow construction paper (or cut them by hand). Label each star with a different numeral from one to ten. Laminate the stars for durability and store them in a string-tie envelope. Invite students to work individually to sequence the stars correctly from one through ten. Then challenge them to sequence the numbers backward and count from ten to one. Tell your Space Ace trainees that counting backward is important practice for the countdown to liftoff!

"Out In Space" Booklets

Each of your Space Ace trainees can review what she's learned about the bodies in space by making an individual "Out In Space" booklet. (You may want to have students complete each page of the booklet in a separate session, rather than all at one time.) In advance prepare shallow pans of yellow, blue, and green tempera paint, as well as a pan of diluted, black tempera paint. Each child will need three sheets of black construction paper, two sheets of blue construction paper, and one sheet of white construction paper—as well as glue, crayons, scissors, a small sheet of foil star stickers, a paintbrush, sponges, and one or two cotton balls. For each child, duplicate the cover and text on page 54. Have each child cut out the cover art on the bold lines and the text strips on the dotted lines. Then invite each child to complete her booklet as follows:

Cover: Glue the cover art to the center of a sheet of black construction paper. Color the picture and write your name on the blank.

Page 1: Use yellow tempera paint to paint a small circle in the center of a sheet of blue construction paper. Press one hand into a pan of yellow tempera paint; then make handprints over the circle to represent the sun's rays. When the paint is dry, glue the text strip that reads "The sun so bright" to the bottom of the page.

Page 2: Peel the foil star stickers from your sheet. Stick them all over a sheet of black construction paper. Glue the text strip that reads "The stars at night" to the bottom of the finished page.

Page 3: Color a large, yellow circle in the center of the sheet of white construction paper. Then dip a paintbrush into a pan of diluted, black tempera paint and paint over the entire page. When the paint is dry, glue the text strip that reads "The moon aglow" to the bottom of the page.

Page 4: Draw a large circle in the center of a sheet of blue construction paper. Use sponges to paint inside the circle with blue and green paint. Then tear off small bits of cotton and glue them on top of the paint to represent clouds. When the paint and glue are dry, glue the text strip that reads "The Earth I know" to the bottom of the page.

When all the pages are finished, stack them in order behind the cover. Add the remaining sheet of black construction paper to the bottom of the stack to serve as a back cover. Staple the pages along the left edge. Encourage little ones to share their booklets and their knowledge about space with their families.

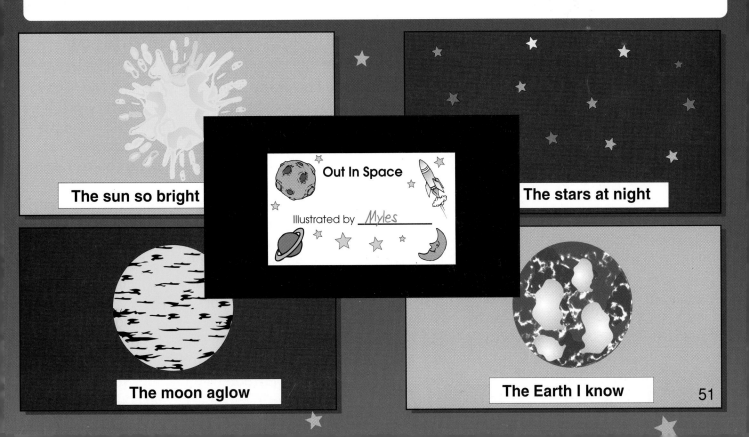

The sun so bright

The stars at night

Out In Space

Illustrated by *Myles*

The moon aglow

The Earth I know

Dress The Part

Your future Space Aces are almost at the end of their training! It's time to fit them with astronaut masks, so they'll be dressed for some fun and far-out adventures. Enlist the help of a couple of parent volunteers to help you prepare the masks. Purchase—or ask volunteers to donate—a class supply of 12-inch, white cake rounds. These are available at party-supply, paper, or craft stores. Use an X-acto® knife to cut each cake round as shown. Use a hole puncher to make one hole in each side of the mask. Thread each end of a 15-inch length of elastic through one hole and tie the elastic securely at each side to create a headband.

For each child, duplicate a copy of the U.S. flag pattern on page 55. Encourage each child to color and cut out his flag; then have him glue it to the front of his mask, above the opening for his face. Write "Space Ace [Child's Name]" on the area below the opening. Invite each child to wear his mask during the activities in "Practice Mission" and "Certified Space Aces."

Practice Mission

Invite youngsters to participate in one final activity before becoming Space Aces—a practice mission! Have youngsters wear their astronaut masks (see "Dress the Part") as they perform the movements to "Space Adventure" on the album, *On The Move With Greg And Steve* (Youngheart Records). This fun movement activity is sure to ignite your little ones' imaginations! If you can't locate the album, have fun making up the movements for an imaginary space journey, such as *get into your space suit, climb aboard the space shuttle, count down to liftoff,* and so on.

Certified Space Aces

At last! Your youngsters have completed all the necessary activities to earn the title "Space Ace!" Duplicate and personalize the award certificate on page 55 for each child. During a ceremony, present each Space Ace with his certificate. For added fun, take a photo of each child wearing his astronaut mask (see "Dress The Part") and holding his certificate. Glue each developed photo to a construction-paper star cutout. Mount the cutouts on a bulletin board with the title "Certified Space Aces." Your shining stars are sure to be proud of their Space Ace accomplishments!

Invite youngsters to put their knowledge into play as they use the class-designed shuttle (from "Engineers At Work" on page 47) in your dramatic play area. Ready for some imaginary space travel? T-minus-10 and counting....

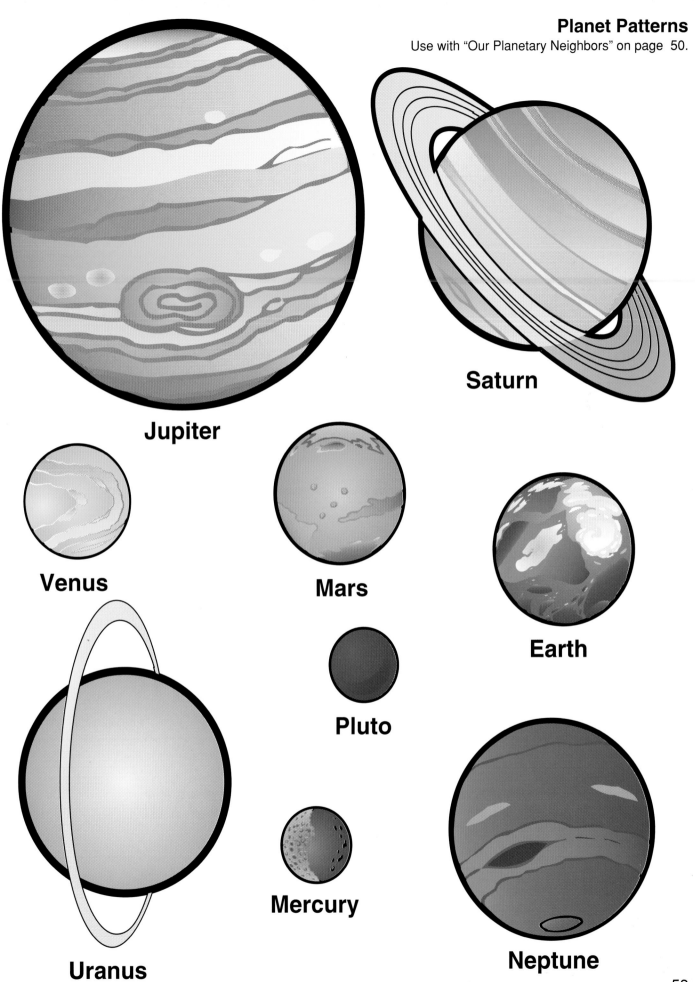

Jupiter

Saturn

Venus

Mars

Earth

Pluto

Uranus

Mercury

Neptune

Booklet Cover And Text

Use with " 'Out In Space' Booklets" on page 51.

Out In Space

Illustrated by _____

©1996 The Education Center, Inc. • *NOVEMBER* • TEC204

The sun so bright

The stars at night

The moon aglow

The Earth I know

©1996 The Education Center, Inc. • *NOVEMBER* • TEC204

Badge
Use with "Getting Ready" on page 46.

Flag Pattern
Use with "Dress The Part" on page 52.

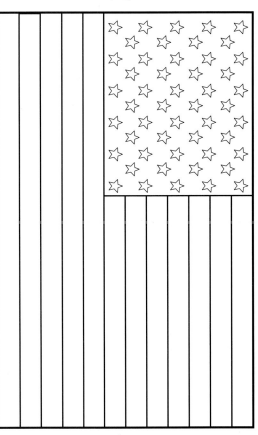

Award Certificate
Use with "Certified Space Aces" on page 52.

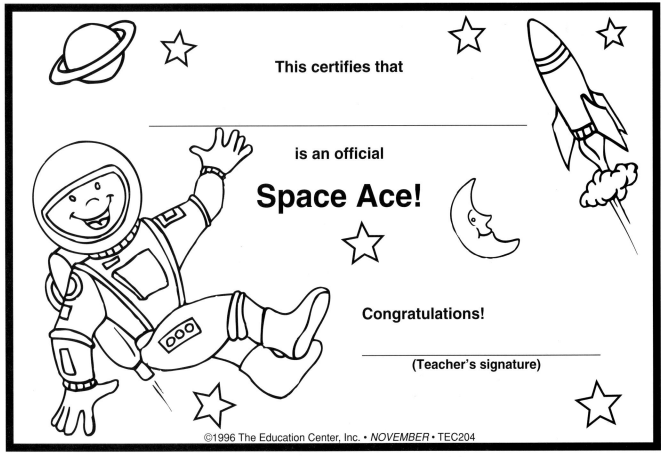

This certifies that

_____

is an official

Space Ace!

Congratulations!

_____
(Teacher's signature)

LET'S TALK TURKEY!

When they get the straight facts on turkeys, your youngsters will have plenty to gobble about at Thanksgiving!

by Mackie Rhodes

WHAT IS IT CALLED?

A male turkey is called a *tom* or a *gobbler*.
A female turkey is called a *hen*.
A newly hatched or young turkey is called a *poult*.

BIRD WORDS

Contrary to common belief, turkeys produce a variety of sounds in addition to the gobble. In fact, the gobble is a seasonal call made by the male turkey and heard typically in late winter and early spring. Describe to your students some of the different sounds produced by turkeys. A newly hatched poult softly *cheeps*. As the chick gets older, it produces a louder *kee-kee-kee* sound. A turkey hen *yelps*. When frightened, a turkey may produce a call similar to its name, *turc-turc*. When strutting, a tom turkey makes a soft *chunk* sound followed by a sharp *gobble*. Using these turkey sounds, play a listening game with your little ones. Produce a sound to represent a poult, hen, tom, or frightened turkey. Encourage your youngsters to identify the kind of turkey that makes that noise. After several rounds, introduce a more challenging game. Ask students to listen carefully as you produce two, three, or four different turkey sounds in sequence. Then invite volunteers to reproduce the sounds in the same sequence. To reinforce the sounds produced by turkeys, sing any or all of these verses.

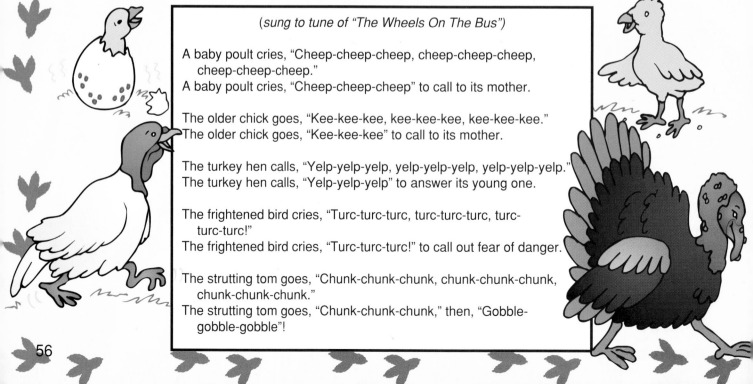

(*sung to tune of "The Wheels On The Bus"*)

A baby poult cries, "Cheep-cheep-cheep, cheep-cheep-cheep,
  cheep-cheep-cheep."
A baby poult cries, "Cheep-cheep-cheep" to call to its mother.

The older chick goes, "Kee-kee-kee, kee-kee-kee, kee-kee-kee."
The older chick goes, "Kee-kee-kee" to call to its mother.

The turkey hen calls, "Yelp-yelp-yelp, yelp-yelp-yelp, yelp-yelp-yelp."
The turkey hen calls, "Yelp-yelp-yelp" to answer its young one.

The frightened bird cries, "Turc-turc-turc, turc-turc-turc, turc-
  turc-turc!"
The frightened bird cries, "Turc-turc-turc!" to call out fear of danger.

The strutting tom goes, "Chunk-chunk-chunk, chunk-chunk-chunk,
  chunk-chunk-chunk."
The strutting tom goes, "Chunk-chunk-chunk," then, "Gobble-
  gobble-gobble"!

TURKEY STRUT

In the world of turkeys, the strut is unique to the male—and so innate that males begin strutting when only a day old! Locate a picture of a strutting male turkey to show your students. Describe the physical features of a turkey in strut: head held high, chin tucked in, feathers puffed, tail fanned, wings lowered, and with a slow, stiff walk. Have your children examine the picture, then position their bodies to resemble (as closely as possible) strutting turkeys. Encourage them to strut around the room as they produce the gobble of a strutting turkey. To give some structure to your little strutters' movements, use masking tape to form several large shapes on the floor. Then invite the children to strut along the outlines of the shapes. If desired, have your little turkeys strut in rhythm to some music.

"WATTLE" YOU KNOW!

Youngsters will enjoy expanding their turkey-related vocabulary as they create their own turkeys with this multisensory activity. Show the children a picture of a turkey. As they examine the picture, name and describe some of the physical characteristics of a turkey's head and neck. The growth of skin above its beak is known as a *snood*. The *wattle* is a piece of skin hanging from a turkey's throat. *Caruncles*, fleshy growths of skin, can be found on the head and neck of a turkey. The skin on a turkey's head is typically red and wrinkled, but a male's skin color can change from red to blue.

After telling students about these turkey features, give each child a copy of the reproducible on page 63. Provide glue, red and blue tissue paper, and play dough. Using the color of his choice, encourage each child to tear his tissue into small pieces. Then have him glue the tissue to the turkey to represent the wrinkled skin and wattle. With the same color play dough, have the child form a snood to glue to his picture. To make caruncles, show him how to squeeze glue drops at random on his turkey's head and neck. If desired, add a wiggle eye. When dry, invite youngsters to take their turkeys home to share with their families. "Wattle" you know! Your amazing little ones will learn some amazing facts about turkeys!

TURKEY TROT

Wild turkeys are quite good runners. With strides up to four feet in length, they can run as fast as 25 miles per hour. While running, the male throws his head back and drags his wings along the ground. Give students an opportunity to participate in a turkey trot with this listening and movement activity. Explain to students that they will pretend to be wild turkeys by scratching the ground with their feet, flapping their arms, and stretching their necks. When you call out, "Trot, turkeys, trot," have each turkey run once around a designated area; then resume his activity of scratching, flapping, and stretching. As long as interest dictates, continue alternating the two activities.

WEATHER BIRD

Can turkey behavior provide reliable weather forecasts? According to some beliefs and superstitions, it can. When turkeys were observed taking dust baths, the Aztecs were sure that rain would soon follow. Some people look for a storm when turkeys stand with their backs to the wind or when they gobble, preen, and then ruffle their feathers. Others expect cold weather to arrive after observing turkeys perched on top of a building. Whether or not turkey behavior can be used to predict the weather, your students will delight in using this weather bird to give the weather report for the the day.

To make the weather bird, duplicate a turkey body, head, beak, and five feathers on desired colors of construction paper using the patterns on pages 64 and 65. Color and cut out the weather pictures on page 65. Glue one picture to each feather as indicated. Assemble the turkey body on a 9" x 12" sheet of tagboard, gluing the body only where indicated. Laminate each piece of the weather board. So that feathers can be inserted, use an X-acto® knife to slit along the top edge of the turkey body. To use, insert the weather feathers into the top of the turkey's body. Each day during the month of November, invite one child to be the weather reporter. Encourage him to carry the weather bird to a window or outdoors to check the weather. Ask him to identify the feather with the picture that best represents the weather. Then have him flip the other feathers around so that only the solid side is visible. Ask the child to share with the class the current weather conditions. Can turkeys forecast the weather? This turkey can!

THE TURKEY SCRATCH

When a turkey is feeding, it searches for food with an established scratch pattern. The mess left by a scratching flock of turkeys makes the feeding area look as though pigs have been rooting through the ground. Have your students practice the turkey's scratch pattern, as indicated in the first verse of this song. Assist them in distinguishing left from right by placing a turkey sticker or stamp on each child's left hand. Then encourage the students to perform the movements to the tune as they role-play turkeys feeding.

(sung to tune of "Short'nin' Bread")

First make a long scratch with the left foot.
Then two short scratches with the right.
Now another long scratch with the left foot.
Head up high. Look left. Look right.

Now bend down your head
And peck, peck, peck.
Peck your food to the left, to the right.

Bend down your head
And peck, peck, peck.
Eat all the food within your sight.

NOTORIOUS NIBBLERS

What would your days be like if the majority of your time was used to search for food and to eat? Wild turkeys know! Turkeys have been called notorious nibblers. They feed along the ground, pecking here and there for acorns, berries, seeds, insects, nuts, and mushrooms. Read aloud the book *Sometimes It's Turkey, Sometimes It's Feathers* by Lorna Balian (Abingdon Press). Discuss the feeding habits of Turkey. Then entice your little ones to become nibbling turkeys with this snacktime activity. On a paper plate for each child, scatter a mixture of crispy rice cereal, small soup crackers, and raisins to represent turkey food. For fun, have the children pretend to be turkeys feeding at the table. Encourage them to bend their heads toward their plates and eat their snacks without using their hands. There will be giggles and gobbles galore!

TURKEY STUFFING

Turkey farmers use specially formulated food to fatten their birds. With this relay game, youngsters will fatten a turkey with a combination of teamwork and speed. Divide your class into several teams of equal numbers. On one end of a field or court, place one pillowcase for each team. At the other end, place the same number of boxes containing a supply of newspapers. Station each team beside a box of papers. Explain that the pillowcase represents a turkey and the newspaper will be used to stuff the turkey. On a signal, each player in turn will take a sheet of newspaper from the box, run to the opposite end of the field, stuff the paper into the turkey, then return to his teammates to tag the next player. Continue in this manner until every team player has had a turn to stuff the turkey.

TERRIFIC TURKEY EGGS

A turkey egg is twice the size of a chicken egg. It has a cream-colored shell with brown speckles. After an incubation period of four weeks, the poult pecks a hole in the shell and hatches out. With this activity your youngsters can make their own speckled turkey eggs. In a shallow tray, spread a thin layer of allspice or cinnamon. Give each student a manila construction-paper egg cutout. Have him randomly dot glue over the surface of his egg using a cotton swab. Then have him turn his egg over and place it on the tray of spice. Encourage the child to gently pat the back of the egg, then pick it up and shake off the excess spice. When the eggs have dried, display them on a nest background titled "Terrific Turkey Eggs."

NEST EGGS

When prompted by her nesting instinct, a wild turkey hen builds her nest from dry leaves on the ground. It takes up to two weeks for a hen to produce a *clutch* of 10–12 eggs. Since more than one hen may share a nest, dozens of eggs may be found in one nest. Use this nesting activity to promote counting instincts in your little ones. To represent turkey nests, place two plastic hoops on the ground. If desired scatter die-cut tissue-paper leaves in the nests. Randomly place four dozen or more large plastic eggs around the room. Pair children; then explain that they will be turkey hens. Assign a pair of hens to each nest. Have each hen look for eggs around the room, bringing them one at a time to her nest until as many as possible have been found. Then ask the hen pairs to sit inside the nests with their eggs. Encourage each to count all the eggs in the nest. After relating each of the amounts to the class, ask which nest contains the most or least number of eggs. Continue play to give each pair of hens the opportunity to satisfy its nesting instincts.

TURKEYS IN A ROW

Wild turkeys travel in flocks often consisting of a hen, her young, and one or two gobblers. Invite youngsters to pretend to be part of a flock of turkeys. Then provide some organization to your flock. In a row, have three children each assume a different position to represent a turkey at rest, standing, or in flight. For example, have the first child sit on the floor with his legs tucked under him, the second child stand with his arms by his sides, and the last child stand with arms outspread. Next ask a volunteer to join the row by duplicating the position of the first child. Have each subsequent volunteer decide the body position he must duplicate in order to continue repetition of the pattern. Proceed in this manner until all the turkeys are in a row. What a well-organized flock of turkeys!

A STRAIGHT DRIVE?

It is nearly impossible to drive a flock of turkeys in a straight line. Ask anyone who has ever tried! To demonstrate how difficult this feat is, have students make their own turkeys to drive—by wind power! Using the pattern on page 65, prepare a turkey-feet cutout from construction paper for each child. Provide each child with that cutout, two 12" x 12" sheets of colored tissue paper, a craft stick with the bottom edge cut straight, and a length of yarn. With the sheets together, have the student fold them in half two times. Starting at the middle of the folded edges, help him gather the paper toward the middle. Place the craft stick—the turkey's head and neck—along the folded edge of paper that does not separate. To attach the craft stick, assist the child in tying the yarn around it at the gathers of the paper. Have him spread the tissue paper above the yarn to represent a turkey plume. Below the yarn on the back of the turkey, show the child how to shape the tissue paper into a hollow-shaped bowl—the turkey's plump body. Glue the turkey-feet cutout to the bottom of the turkey. If desired, use a marker to make eyes and a beak on the craft stick to resemble a turkey face. Near the edge of a table, encourage the child to balance his turkey so that it is facing away from him. Have him place his chin at table level and blow gently into the hollowed bowl of the turkey body to make his turkey move. Challenge him to blow, or "drive," the turkey as straight as possible. Can he do it? With turkeys going this way and that, youngsters will experience what a real turkey drive must be like.

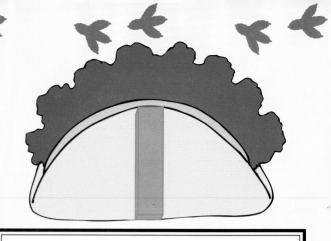

JUST PLAIN GOOD FOR YOU

With the heightened awareness of low-fat food options, turkey meat has become increasingly popular and in demand. Not only is turkey readily marketed and relatively inexpensive, but it can be purchased in a variety of forms and preparations and is quite tasty. To give your little ones a taste of turkey, have them create these turkey tacos for snacktime. Give each child a flour tortilla, a slice of turkey luncheon meat, a lettuce leaf, and a strip of cheese. Have him place the turkey on the tortilla and fold it in half. Then show him how to put the lettuce into the tortilla so that it resembles the plume of a turkey. Guide the child to place the strip of cheese on top of the tortilla to represent a turkey head and neck. When the turkey taco is ready, encourage each youngster to gobble his up!

TURKEY FEATHERS

The breed of a turkey determines its feather coloring. The most common, the *Bronze* turkey, sports white-tipped feathers with red, green, brown, and black hues. Other turkey breeds may also have multicolored feathers or may be almost entirely one color, such as black or white. To promote exploration, self-expression, and creativity in your little ones, place a quantity of feathers in various colors and shapes in a large box. Prompt students to use the feathers to create shapes, designs, or letters on the floor. Suggest that the feathers be used to practice writing at the sand table. Invite young-sters to dip feathers in paint or colored water to use for drawing at the easel. Encourage them to make patterns with the various colors or sizes of feathers. Engage students in making craft projects with some of the feathers. With feath-ers and a light touch of encouragement, each student's creativity will take flight and soar!

A FLOCK OF GOOD BOOKS ABOUT TURKEYS

Sometimes It's Turkey, Sometimes It's Feathers
Written by Lorna Balian
Published by Abingdon Press

A Turkey For Thanksgiving
Written by Eve Bunting
Published by Clarion Books

'Twas The Night Before Thanksgiving
Written by Dav Pilkey
Published by Orchard Books

One Tough Turkey: A Thanksgiving Story
Written by Steven Kroll
Published by Holiday House, Inc.

Farmer Goff And His Turkey Sam
Written by Brian Schatell
Published by J. B. Lippincott

Turkey Head Pattern
Use with " 'Wattle' You Know" on page 57.

Weather Bird Patterns
Use with "Weather Bird" on page 58.

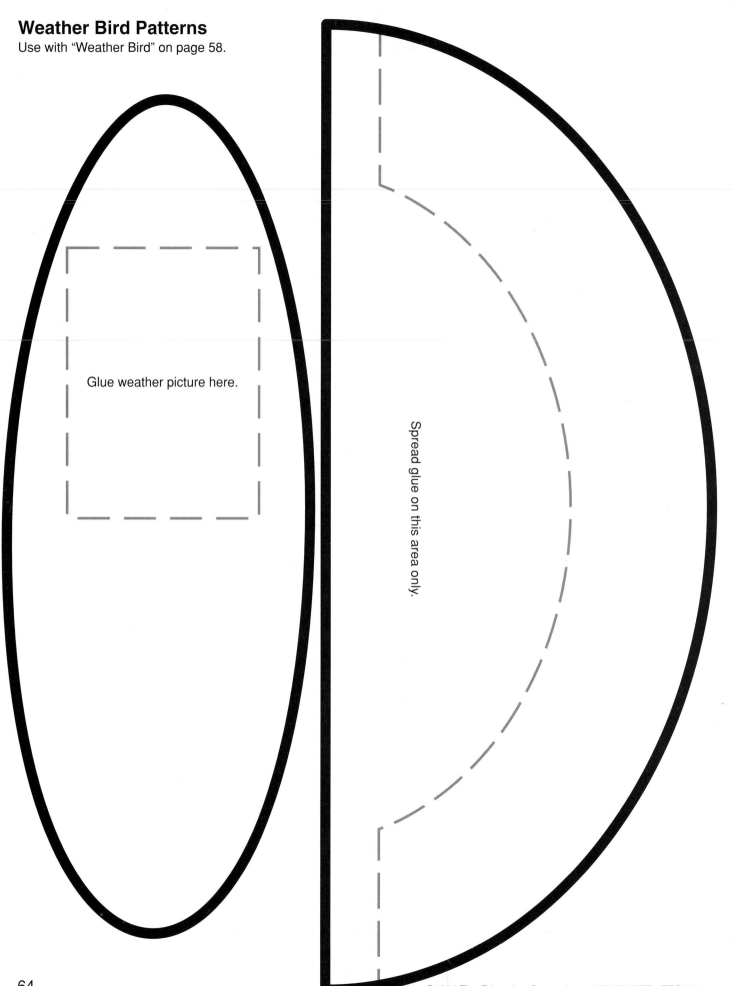

Glue weather picture here.

Spread glue on this area only.

sunny

cloudy

rainy

snowy

windy

beak

head/neck

Turkey Feet Pattern
Use with "A Straight Drive?" on page 61.

The First American Thanksgiving

Share information about the customs and lifestyles of the Native American people of the eastern woodlands and the early Pilgrim settlers with your youngsters. Then delight them with activities that highlight the friendship forged between these two groups and the resulting celebration—the first American Thanksgiving!

ideas contributed by Deborah Burleson, Lucia Kemp Henry, and Mackie Rhodes

A Longhouse Is A Lot Of House!

In this measurement activity, youngsters will go to great lengths to experience the distance covered by a Native American longhouse. In advance measure and mark a distance of 100 feet along your school's sidewalk or playing field. During group time, explain that many of the Native Americans of the eastern woodlands lived in homes called *longhouses*. The houses were given their name because they were long—sometimes 100 feet or longer! Take students to the premeasured area so they can see just how long 100 feet is. Invite them to lie down head-to-toe to form a line along the marked distance. While they are lying on the ground, count to determine how many children it takes to cover a distance of 100 feet. If necessary, ask children who were counted first to lie down at the other end of the line until the entire distance is covered. Then have students discuss what they think it would be like to live in a longhouse.

A Typical Day

Use this call-response song to familiarize little ones with some of the routine activities of Native Americans in the early 1600s. Before singing each call verse, whisper the action from that verse to a different child. Encourage the child to perform movements to represent that action while the class sings his name in the response. Repeat the song until every student has had a turn to perform a movement.

Who Is In The Longhouse?
(sung to the tune of "Mary Wore A Red Dress")

Who is [in the longhouse, longhouse, longhouse]?
Who is [in the longhouse],
[Sweeping the floor]?

[Child's name] is [in the longhouse, longhouse, longhouse]?
[Child's name] is [in the longhouse],
[Sweeping the floor]!

Each time the song is repeated, replace the underlined phrase with one of the italicized phrases below. Then choose one of the action phrases that follow for the last line of each verse.

- *in the longhouse* .... building a fire; eating corn
- *by the warm fire* .... cooking beans; sewing clothes
- *in the village* .... playing ball; weaving baskets
- *in the big field* .... planting seeds; gathering squash
- *at the river* .... catching fish; taking a bath
- *in the forest* .... chopping wood; gathering nuts

Shake It To The Beat

Have students make their own versions of a Native American rattle and water drum.

To make a rattle for each child, collect a small frozen-juice can and its lid. Put a variety of bean and corn seeds into a container. Then prepare a  tray of paint and several different sponge shapes. Have each child sponge-paint designs on a strip of construction paper cut to fit around his can. When the paint dries, glue the paper around the can. Have the student place a few spoonfuls of the seed mixture in his can; then glue the lid in place. When the glue dries, encourage student partners to take turns creating and reproducing simple rhythmic patterns using their rattles.

To prepare a water drum, collect a large shortening or margarine container with a plastic lid for each child. Encourage each youngster to use crayons or markers to create designs and patterns on a sheet of construction paper cut to fit around his container. Wrap the paper snugly around the container; then glue it in place. Clip clothespins around the container's rim to hold the paper until the glue dries. Then partially fill each container with water and place the lid on it. In turn have each youngster beat his drum for the class. Encourage students to listen to and compare the different pitches created by the drums.

Put the rattles and drums aside to be used again in "A Feast Of Thanks" on page 71.

Story Belt

Have your students create their own Native American *wampum* belts—belts made of shell beads. To make imitation wampum beads, mix one-half cup of rubbing alcohol, a few drops of food coloring, and one cup of small pasta shells in a separate container for each color desired. When they are thoroughly covered with the colored mixture, remove them from the liquid; then spread them out on paper towels to dry overnight. Explain to students that the Native Americans sewed wampum beads onto belts to record stories. Invite each child to make her own wampum belt on a 4" x 18" strip of tagboard by gluing the colored shells onto her strip in the form of characters or designs. When the glue dries, have the child write or dictate a sentence about her wampum belt on a strip of paper. Glue the paper strip to the back of her belt. Use a hole puncher to make a hole in each end of the belt. Thread a length of yarn through each hole in the belt and tie it securely. Tie the belt around the child's waist. Invite each youngster in turn to tell the class about her wampum belt. Afterward have the children remove the belts and put them aside for use in "A Feast Of Thanks" on page 71.

The sun helps things grow.   Amber

A Trip To Remember

Use a class-made model of the *Mayflower* and lots of descriptive language to help your youngsters imagine the Pilgrim children's voyage to the New World. To learn about some of the Pilgrims' experiences, use the sections regarding the *Mayflower* and the Pilgrims' voyage in *...If You Sailed On The Mayflower In 1620* or *The Pilgrims' First Thanksgiving,* both by Ann McGovern (Scholastic Inc.).

To make a model of the *Mayflower,* obtain a large appliance box, two brooms, and four poster boards. In advance use a utility knife to cut the box to resemble a ship. Provide several trays of tempera paint and some paintbrushes. Have one small group of children at a time paint the box. When the paint dries, cut one slit near the top of a box end and another slit at the bottom directly below the first slit. In the same manner,

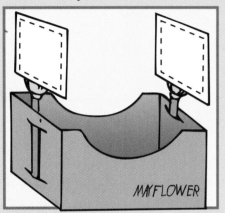

cut slits on the opposite end of the box. Create a mast for a sail by sliding a broom handle through one slit, then through the other, at each box end. To make a sail for each mast, staple two sheets of white poster board together along three edges. Then slip the open ends of the poster boards over the brooms. Print the name *"Mayflower"* on the side of the ship with a wide permanent marker.

Using the information from the books, describe what the voyage must have been like for the children on the *Mayflower*. Then invite small groups of students to role-play Pilgrim children sailing to the New World.

Miniature Mayflower

Have little ones make miniature models of the *Mayflower* to take home and share with their families. Collect a class supply of walnut-shell halves and small baby-food jars with lids. For each child, cut a small sail from white construction paper; then cut a circle slightly smaller than the opening of the jar from blue construction paper to represent the sea. Have the child glue the sail cutout to one end of a 1 1/2" length of craft stick. Give the child a small amount of play dough to press into the walnut shell. Then have him push the craft stick into the play dough. Help the child glue the walnut half to the sea cutout so that it resembles a ship on water. When that glue dries, have the child place a few drops of glue in the bottom of his baby-food jar. Help him place the entire ship-and-water assembly into the jar over the glue; then have him place the lid on the jar. When the glue in their miniature models is dry, encourage youngsters to take the models home and tell their families what they have learned about the *Mayflower's* voyage.

Land, Ho!

When your students make these body posters, they will get caught up in the excitement of learning more about the Pilgrims. In advance cut four child-length pieces of white butcher paper. Have the students discuss how the Pilgrim children must have felt when the *Mayflower* finally made landfall in the New World. Ask them to talk about some of the things the children may have done at that time. Did they jump up and down with joy? Did they run excitedly along the beach? After the discussion, divide the students into four groups. Have one child from each  group lie on the sheet of butcher paper. Encourage him to position his body to represent a Pilgrim child who is jumping, running, or showing excitement. Trace that child's body onto the paper with a marker. Then have students examine pictures of Pilgrim children and their clothing in *The Pilgrims' First Thanksgiving* by Ann McGovern (Scholastic Inc.). Ask each group to work together to embellish their Pilgrim-body outline with facial features and clothing using a variety of craft items. Invite each group to dictate what they think their Pilgrim child would have said when the ship landed. Write the dictated sentences on speech bubbles. Then display each poster and its speech bubble with the title "Land, Ho!"

All In A Pilgrim's Day

Youngsters will delight in pretending to perform Pilgrim jobs with this song that describes some of the typical activities of the early settlers. Before singing the song, read aloud or paraphrase Kate Waters's *Sarah Morton's Day: A Day In The Life Of A Pilgrim Girl* and *Samuel Eaton's Day: A Day In The Life Of A Pilgrim Boy* (both published by Scholastic Inc.). While singing the song, encourage students to perform actions to represent the job described in each verse.

This Is The Way We Stir The Pudding

(sung to the tune of "Here We Go 'Round The Mulberry Bush")

This is the way we [stir the pudding, stir the pudding, stir the pudding].
This is the way we [stir the pudding]
All in a Pilgrim's day!

Each time the song is repeated, replace the underlined words with one of the following: *knead the bread, feed the hens, milk the goats, fetch the water, gather the wood, hoe the garden, pull the corn, husk the corn, catch a fish,* and *pick up nuts.*

A Friendship Is Formed

Help youngsters begin to understand how the Native Americans and Pilgrim settlers learned to live and grow together. Explain to students that the Pilgrims encountered many hardships when they arrived in the New World. The Native Americans, especially one named Squanto, became friends with the settlers and taught them many ways to survive. The Pilgrims were taught several different ways to plant and grow crops for food. One popular trio of crops—corn, beans, and squash—were planted together on little hills in the field. The corn grew upright, while the bean vines twined around the cornstalks, and the squash vines grew out along the ground to choke out weeds. This combination of plants was sometimes referred to as "Three Sisters." Invite little ones to perform the motions to this poem about how corn, beans, and squash were planted and grown together.

Fabulous Foods

With this matching game, students can satisfy their appetites for more knowledge about the foods introduced to the Pilgrims by the Native Americans. Make two copies of the food pictures on pages 72, 73, and 74; then set the original pages aside for use in "If I Were At The First Thanksgiving" on page 71. Color the two sets of pictures so that they are identical. Cut the cards apart. Mount each picture on a slightly larger piece of tagboard; then laminate them for durability. Spread the cards out facedown on a table or the floor. Prior to playing the game, explain to students that the cards show different kinds of foods that Native Americans helped the Pilgrims to grow or find. Then invite a pair of children to play a matching game with the food cards. To play, the children take turns looking for a match by selecting two cards at a time. Continue play until all the food cards have been matched. Then invite another pair of students to play so that all the children have the opportunity to play the game.

Three Sisters

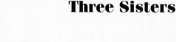

Corn, beans, and squash	*Hold up three fingers.*
Help us grow strong.	*Flex arms in a strongman pose.*
Plant them together	*Pretend to plant three seeds on hand.*
And you can't go wrong!	*Shake head back and forth.*
The corn grows up straight.	*Stand straight with arms at sides.*
The beans twine around.	*Circle index finger in the air.*
The squash spreads out wide	*Stretch arms out wide.*
And shades the rich ground.	*Shade head with both hands.*
Cook corn, beans, and squash	*Hold up one, two, then three fingers.*
When you want healthy food.	*Rub tummy and smile.*
They taste oh so nice,	*Make smacking noise with mouth.*
And they make you feel good!	*Flex arms, grin, and nod head.*

—Lucia Kemp Henry

If I Were At The First Thanksgiving

Your students can take an imaginary step back in time when they create these books about the first Thanksgiving meal. Duplicate a class supply of the food pictures on pages 72, 73, and 74. Then make four copies of page 75 for each child. Explain to students that the early settlers and their Native American friends decided to have a large celebration to give thanks for their homes, their food, and each other. Using a set of the food cards from "Fabulous Foods" on page 70, review the types of foods that the Native Americans and Pilgrims ate. Tell the students that many of these foods were served at the first Thanksgiving. Encourage them to decide which foods they would have eaten at that meal. Then have each child select and color four of the foods from his set of food pictures. Have him cut the colored food pictures apart. On each of his book pages, have the child glue a food picture; then have him write or dictate an ending for the sentence. Place the completed book pages between two construction-paper covers. Staple the pages together along the left edge. Print "If I Were At The First Thanksgiving…" on the front cover. If desired, invite students to color and cut apart the remainder of their food pictures. Encourage each youngster to take his book and extra food pictures home to share with his family.

A Feast Of Thanks

Youngsters can taste a sampling of foods used by the Native Americans and Pilgrims at the first Thanksgiving feast during this class feast of thanks. In advance ask parents to donate foods represented by the food cards in "Fabulous Foods" on page 70. Arrange for volunteers to help prepare these foods for the feast. Prior to the feast, ask each child to name something he would give thanks for if he had participated in the first Thanksgiving. Then invite students to wear their wampum belts (made in "Story Belt" on page 67) for the feast. Offer a small serving of each type of food to each student. When every student has the foods of his choice on his plate, invite all the children to enjoy their meals, just as the first Thanksgiving participants did so many years ago. Following the feast, continue the celebration with music and dance. Play some rhythmic music and invite youngsters to dance and to play their rattles or drums (made in "Shake It To The Beat" on page 67). Afterward encourage students to take their belts and instruments home to use during their own Thanksgiving celebrations.

Feast On These Books About The First Thanksgiving
Published by Scholastic Inc.

The Story Of The First Thanksgiving
Written by Elaine Raphael and Don Bolognese

Friendship's First Thanksgiving
Written by William Accorsi

The Thanksgiving Story
Written by Alice Dalgliesh

Food Pictures

Use with "Fabulous Foods" on page 70 and "If I Were At The First Thanksgiving" on page 71.

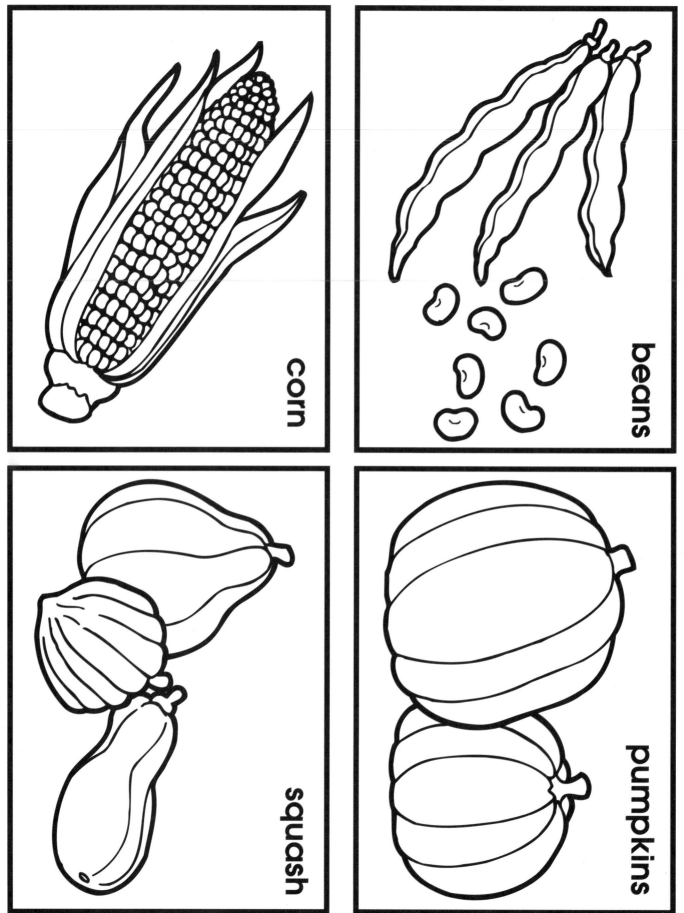

corn

beans

squash

pumpkins

Food Pictures

Use with "Fabulous Foods" on page 70 and "If I Were At The First Thanksgiving" on page 71.

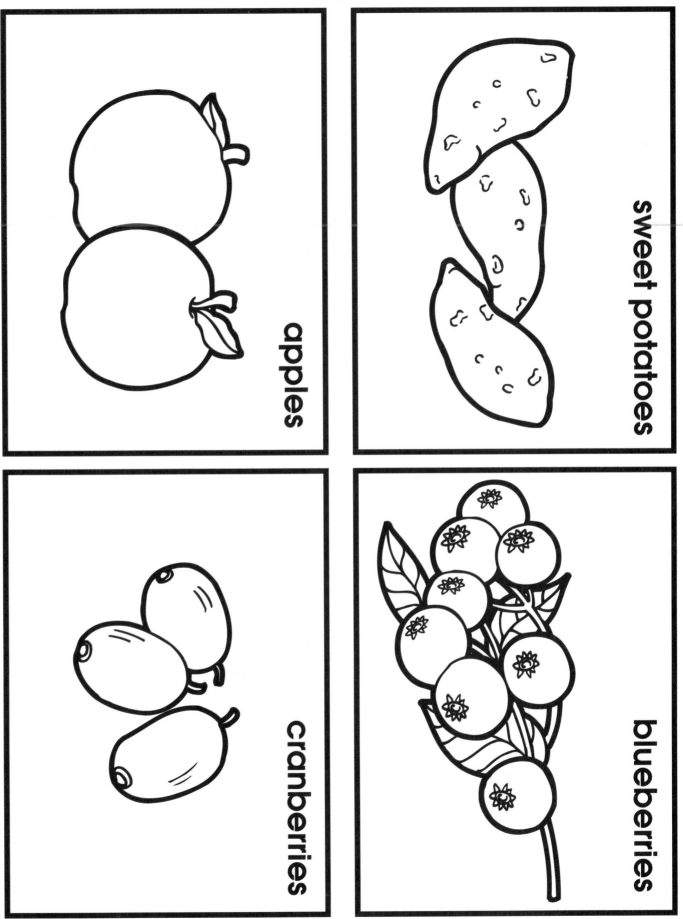

apples

sweet potatoes

cranberries

blueberries

Food Pictures

Use with "Fabulous Foods" on page 70 and "If I Were At The First Thanksgiving" on page 71.

blackberries

sunflower seeds

nuts

maple syrup

I would eat _____.

Note To The Teacher: Use with "If I Were At The First Thanksgiving" on page 71.

Think Thanks!

These treats, trimmings, and times to reflect will have youngsters thinking thanks for the many terrific things in their lives.

ideas contributed by Deborah Burleson, Lucia Kemp Henry, and Mackie Rhodes

A-Tisket, A-Tasket, We're Gonna Fill A Basket!

Weave a home-school connection by inviting parents and students to donate food for a giving basket. In advance, arrange to distribute food donations to a charitable organization or a needy family. Obtain a large basket or decorate a box to resemble a basket. Embellish the basket with ribbon, bows, and other trimmings. Then duplicate the parent letter on page 82 for each child.

Ask students to think about the many foods they eat each day. Encourage them to name some of their favorite foods. Do they feel thankful when they eat their favorites? Tell them that some children and their families do not have very much food or very many different foods to eat. Then show them the basket and explain that it is a giving basket—that the class will collect food in the basket to give to people in need. The food will be given to a family or families in time for Thanksgiving. Ask the students to tell their families about the giving basket. Provide each student with a copy of the parent letter to take home. As each child brings in a donation, tell him how much his contribution to the giving basket is appreciated. To keep youngsters interested in filling the basket, use the contents of the basket for the activities in "Taking Inventory."

Taking Inventory

Keep little ones "ac-count-able" for the contents of the giving basket in "A-Tisket, A-Tasket, We're Gonna Fill A Basket" by having them take a daily inventory. Each day encourage a small group of students to empty the basket. Have them sort the items from the basket into different categories. Encourage the students to use various criteria for sorting, such as *food types* (beans, tomatoes, corn) or *package types* (cans, boxes, bags). List the different categories chosen by the group on a sheet of chart paper. Have the youngsters count the number of items in each category. Write the total of each one beside its corresponding category on the chart. Afterwards help the students place the items back into the basket one at a time, counting each one aloud. Write the total number of items at the bottom of the chart paper and circle that number. Each day compare the total number of items to the number from the previous day. On the last collection day, count all of the items aloud with the class. Return the items to the giving basket; then thank each child for helping to fill and keep count of the foods in the basket. After the basket of food is delivered, be sure to share with students the thanks offered by its recipients.

Sing A Song Of Thanks

Teach youngsters a new way to express their thanks—with the hand sign for *thank you*. Then use the sign each time these words are sung in this song. Follow the sign with the other hand gestures for each line.

Thank You, Thank You; This We Say

(sung to the tune of "Twinkle, Twinkle, Little Star")

Thank you for the earth and sky. — *Form circle with fingertips; then point to sky.*
Thank you for the birds that fly. — *Flap arms.*
Thank you for the food we grow. — *Cup hands together; then slide one arm upward as if to grow.*

Thank you for the streams that flow. — *Flutter fingers as hands move to side.*
Thank you, thank you; this we say: — *Point to lips.*
Thanks for all we have today! — *Spread arms out wide.*

Encourage youngsters to spend time with their parents completing a personalized song of thanks. Duplicate the song on page 83 for each child to take home. Explain to students that their parents or other family members can help them complete each line of the song. After filling in all the blanks, students can sing the song with their families, using the hand sign for *thank you* each time those words are sung.

Ann is thankful for Daddy because he takes care of her.

A Big Book Of Thanks

Little ones can show thanks in a big way when they help make this class book. Refer to the song "Thank You, Thank You; This We Say" to initiate a discussion with students about the many things for which they are thankful. Encourage the children to consider the places they go, the things they do and have, and the people they spend time with as they brainstorm during the discussion. Then give each child a 12" x 18" sheet of white construction paper. Have him illustrate one person or thing for which he is thankful on his paper. Ask him to dictate a completion to the sentence, "[Child's name] is thankful for [person or thing] because _____." Write the completed sentence on his paper. Then assemble all the papers between two construction-paper covers. Staple the book together along the left edge; then write the title "A Big Book Of Thanks" on the front cover. Invite small groups of children to share the book with one another.

Let's Exercise Some Gratitude!

Invite youngsters to join in these exercises to increase their awareness of and appreciation for their wonderful bodies. Explain to students that each exercise is named for something related to Thanksgiving. After performing the exercises, ask each child to name a part of his body for which he is thankful and to tell why.

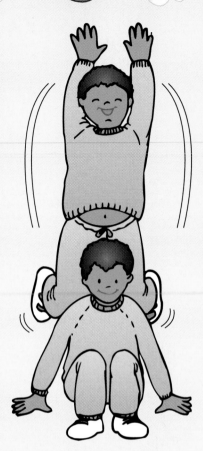

- *Mayflower* **Maneuver:** Students lean back and forth, then side to side.
- **Pilgrim Pop-ups:** Students crouch down low, then jump up as high as they can.
- **Native American Arm Bends:** Students alternately stretch and flex their arms.
- **Settlers' Sit-ups:** Student partners take turns performing sit-ups.
- **Squanto Squeeze:** Students spread arms to sides, then wrap them tightly around their chests.
- **Turkey Trot:** Students run in place.
- **Plymouth Rock:** Students perform free-form movements to music.

A Corny Way To Be Thankful

Little ones will enjoy making "corn-y" expressions of thanks during this hot potato–style game. In advance, purchase an ear of sweet corn. Gather several musical selections to be played during the game. Prior to beginning this activity, find out how many students eat corn. Explain that corn has been a traditional Thanksgiving food since the very first celebration in America.

Then tell students that they will play a game using an ear of corn. To play the game, have students sit in a circle. Explain that they will pass the ear of corn around the circle while the music plays. When the music stops, the child holding the ear of corn will complete the last line of this rhyme with words of his choice. Continue play until every child has had a turn to complete the rhyme.

I'm Thankful

I'm thankful for corn and for bugs I can shoo!
I'm thankful for dirt and for big globs of glue.
I'm thankful for gum and for rocks in my shoe.
I'm thankful for these and for _____, too!

Books To Be Thankful For

Treat youngsters to these literature picks to highlight the spirit of Thanksgiving. Then send a copy of the bookmark on page 82 home with each child to encourage reading together as a family.

Over The River And Through The Woods
illustrated by John Steven Gurney (Scholastic Inc.)

Following some joyous choruses of this Thanksgiving favorite, invite little ones to create their own version of a horse-drawn sleigh. First read the song aloud; then sing it with your students several times. Have a wagon available for youngsters to use as a sleigh. Or make a sleigh from a large box with a rope handle looped through two holes at one end. Arrange an obstacle course using cones, furniture, and a Hula-Hoop® or two to represent features of the terrain described in the song. Encourage small groups of children to ride and maneuver the makeshift sleigh through the obstacle course. Suggest that the children take turns pulling and riding in the sleigh. Give each small group of children an opportunity to use the sleigh.

A
Healthy
Serving
Of Thanks!
by Amber

Thanksgiving At The Tappletons'
by Eileen Spinelli (J. B. Lippincott Junior Books)

After hearing this humorous story about one family's Thanksgiving fiasco, youngsters will delight in creating these paper-plate books. Read the book aloud to students, helping them identify the absurdities in the story. Then, on four separate white paper plates, have each child draw a picture of a person or an activity for which he is thankful. Encourage him to write or dictate a sentence about each picture. Arrange the illustrated plates between two paper-plate covers so that the illustrations are all right-side-up. Use a hole puncher to make two holes through the plates along the rims near the tops of the pictures. Thread a short length of yarn through each set of holes and tie it. On the front cover, write the title "A Healthy Serving Of Thanks!" Encourage students to take their books home to share with their families.

Thanksgiving Treat
by Catherine Stock (Macmillan Publishing Company)

Your students will be ready to lend a helping hand with their own families' Thanksgiving Day preparations after hearing this story. Prior to reading the story, duplicate page 84 on white construction paper for each child. Prepare a tray of tempera paint mixed with a small amount of dishwashing liquid. Read the story aloud to your youngsters. Afterwards engage them in a discussion about the many things their families do to prepare for Thanksgiving. List these things on a sheet of chart paper. Ask students to name some of the things they can do to be helpful during the preparations. Then have each child dip his hand in the tray of paint and make a handprint on his copy of page 84. When the paint dries, encourage each child to take his paper home and have his family help him complete the sentence. Remind students to try to be helpful on Thanksgiving Day.

Dear Parent

On Thanksgiving Day, I can help —

Thanksgiving Trimmings And Treats

Youngsters will enjoy preparing these decorations and dishes for a little taste of Thanksgiving.

Popping With Thanks

"Thanks!" will be popping up everywhere when youngsters make these pop-up cards to express their appreciation for the people and things in their lives. For each child, duplicate the pop-up card pattern on page 85 and trim along the straight dotted line. Have him color the letters in the word "Thanks!" Encourage the child to cut pictures from magazines and catalogs to represent things or people for which he is thankful. Have him glue the pictures in the boxes indicated on his paper. Then cut each child's paper on the curved dotted line. Help the child glue the edges of his paper onto a sheet of construction paper, being careful not to glue the pop-up section. When the glue dries, fold the construction paper in half, pulling the pop-up section forward. On the front of the card, write "For these things, [child's name] gives…." When the card is opened, "Thanks!" will pop up at the cardholder. Encourage students to share their cards with one another, then with family members at home.

Seeded Placemats

As youngsters create these seed design placemats, remind them of the role the Native Americans played in teaching the Pilgrims how to plant and grow crops. In advance, collect a variety of seeds to represent plants that the Native Americans helped Pilgrims to grow, such as seeds from corn, pumpkins, beans, and sunflowers. For each child, cut a 9" x 12" sheet of construction paper in half. To make a placemat, glue each paper-half to the end of a 12" x 18" sheet of construction paper in a contrasting color. Then have the student create designs or patterns by gluing seeds to the sides of his placemat. Put the completed placemats aside for later use in "A Taste Of Thanksgiving" on page 81.

Pleasing Place Cards

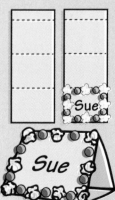

Invite your students to use some foods commonly eaten by the early settlers and Native Americans to make place cards for your Thanksgiving table. To prepare, put dried or fresh cranberries and popped popcorn into separate containers. For each child, cut a 6" x 9" piece of tagboard. Refer to the provided diagram to crease the tagboard cards as indicated. Then write each student's name on his card as shown. Have him glue some popcorn and cranberries around his name. When the glue dries, fold the place card along the creases, and tape the end in place. Set the completed place cards aside to be used in "A Taste Of Thanksgiving" on page 81.

A Taste Of Thanksgiving

Have youngsters help create some of these tasty treats; then add a few of your own favorites to provide a tantalizing taste of Thanksgiving. Set tables with the placemats and place cards made in "Seeded Placemats" and "Pleasing Place Cards" on page 80. Serve each child a cup of cranberry juice with his plate of treats. Enjoy!

Fry Bread

2 cups self-rising flour
1 cup milk
cooking oil

Mix the flour and milk in a large bowl, adding flour as necessary to form a dough. Flatten small amounts of the dough into patties. Using a wok or an electric skillet set at 400°F, brown the bread patties in hot oil. Drain the cooked bread on a paper towel. Serve the warm bread with butter, jam, or cinnamon sugar. Makes approximately 24 small servings of bread.

Sweet Potato Pudding

4 or 5 medium eggs, slightly beaten
4 cups canned sweet potatoes
1 cup brown sugar or honey
1 12-oz. can evaporated milk
1 1/2 teaspoons cinnamon

1 teaspoon salt
1 teaspoon ginger
1/2 teaspoon ground cloves
marshmallows (optional)

Combine all the ingredients, except the marshmallows, and mix well. Pour the mixture into a buttered dish. Bake at 350°F for 45 minutes to 1 hour—until a knife inserted in the center comes out clean. If desired, top the mixture with marshmallows; then return it to the oven until the marshmallows are browned. When cooled, serve the pudding with graham crackers.

Cranapple Cubes

1 16-ounce can cranberry sauce
1 cup chunky applesauce
1 cup plain yogurt

Pour the ingredients into a large bowl and mix them together with a mixer set on low speed for one minute. Pour the mixture into ice-cube trays. Cover the trays with foil; then push a Popsicle® stick through the foil into each cup. Place the trays in a freezer overnight. Pop the cranapple cubes out of the trays and serve them.

Parent Letter
Use with "A-Tisket, A-Tasket, We're Gonna Fill A Basket!" on page 76.

Dear Parent,

As part of our focus on Thanksgiving, our class is collecting nonperishable food items to fill a giving basket. The basket of food will be donated to a needy family in time for Thanksgiving. As the food is collected, our class will inventory the contents of the basket to practice our counting and categorizing skills. Your contribution in this effort will be greatly appreciated. If you can, please send a nonperishable food item to school with your child by _____.

(date)

Thank you!

Bookmark
Use with "Books To Be Thankful For" on page 79.

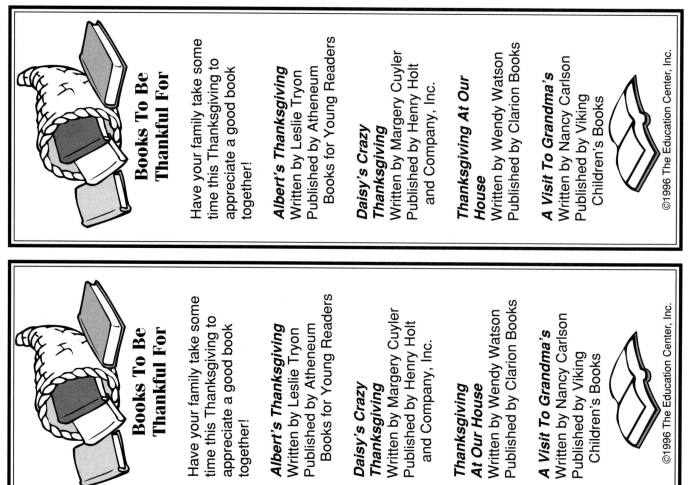

Books To Be Thankful For

Have your family take some time this Thanksgiving to appreciate a good book together!

Albert's Thanksgiving
Written by Leslie Tryon
Published by Atheneum Books for Young Readers

Daisy's Crazy Thanksgiving
Written by Margery Cuyler
Published by Henry Holt and Company, Inc.

Thanksgiving At Our House
Written by Wendy Watson
Published by Clarion Books

A Visit To Grandma's
Written by Nancy Carlson
Published by Viking Children's Books

©1996 The Education Center, Inc.

Books To Be Thankful For

Have your family take some time this Thanksgiving to appreciate a good book together!

Albert's Thanksgiving
Written by Leslie Tryon
Published by Atheneum Books for Young Readers

Daisy's Crazy Thanksgiving
Written by Margery Cuyler
Published by Henry Holt and Company, Inc.

Thanksgiving At Our House
Written by Wendy Watson
Published by Clarion Books

A Visit To Grandma's
Written by Nancy Carlson
Published by Viking Children's Books

©1996 The Education Center, Inc.

Dear Parent,

Our class has been learning about all the things that we are thankful for. Please help your child create a personalized song of thanks by completing the lines to the song below. The song can be sung to the tune of "Twinkle, Twinkle, Little Star." To add variety, have your child use the hand sign for the words *thank you* each time they appear in the song.

Thank you for the _____ I see.

Thank you for the _____ for me.

Thank you for the _____ I know.

Thanks for _____. I love it (or him/her) so!

Thank you, thank you; this I say;

Thanks for all I have today!

Thank you.

Note To The Teacher: Use this parent letter with "Sing A Song Of Thanks" on page 77.

Dear Parent,

Thanksgiving Day brings a lot of excitement, along with the large amount of work necessary to prepare for your family celebration. Before the preparations begin, please decide with your child a way in which he can help. Then complete the sentence. Encourage your child to help during the preparations as stated.

A Helping Hand

On Thanksgiving Day, I can help_____

_____.

Note To The Teacher: Use with *Thanksgiving Treat* on page 79. Have the child make his handprint at the bottom of the page.

©1996 The Education Center, Inc. • *NOVEMBER* • TEC204

Animals In Winter

When fall is all around and hints of winter soon appear,
The animals must get ready for the coldest time of year!

This unit is packed with multidisciplinary ideas, including science, poetry, and language arts. Use the ideas in this unit to introduce your youngsters to some of the habits and habitats of animals in winter.

ideas contributed by Lucia Kemp Henry and Jan Trautman

Winter Is Coming

Begin your unit with this poem that describes the different ways in which wild animals prepare for the cold winter months. In advance, prepare the animal patterns (pages 93 and 95) for flannelboard use. (First duplicate pages 94 and 96 for later use.) After modeling their use, have your youngsters take turns manipulating the pieces as you all read/recite the poem together.

Winter is coming!
The animals know
That the plants and trees
Might be covered in snow.

Winter is coming!
The cold, snowy kind.
Soon food and warm places
Will be quite hard to find.

Winter is coming!
Some animals go
To places down south
Where there isn't much snow.
(Display geese.)

Winter is coming!
And there's a time crunch!
To save acorns and nuts
For a winter-time lunch.
(Display chipmunk and squirrel.)

Winter is coming!
Some animals sleep
In a cave or a den
Or a burrow, down deep.
(Display bear and groundhog.)

Winter is coming!
Some animals know
That *they'll* still find food
So they don't mind the snow.
(Display fox and otter.)

Winter is coming!
And I'll stay right here
To help feed the birds
Through this cold time of year!
(Display birds at the bird feeder.)

—by Lucia Kemp Henry

Dear Rebecca, Winter Is Here

Written by Jean Craighead George
Published by HarperCollins Publishers

Winter in June? Well, not really. But Rebecca learns from her grandmother that while she is cooling off under the hose on a warm summer day, the circle of seasons is already rolling toward winter. And with winter comes change— changes in Rebecca and her grandmother, *and* in nature all around. As you share this book, encourage your youngsters to be on the lookout for animals in the story. Ask them to look and listen carefully to find out what each animal does. As each animal is highlighted in the text, invite your youngsters to dramatize each animal's behavior, then return to their places to continue the story.

What About Us?

Where winter is concerned, not all geographical locations are created equal! Encourage your little ones to describe what winter is like in your area of the country. Write their responses on a large sheet of light blue paper, leaving wide margins around the edges. Then ask youngsters how your type of winter weather affects the animals that live in your area. Also write those responses on the chart. Then put the chart paper in your art center. As children visit the center, invite them to decorate the chart using various art supplies such as stickers, rubber stamps, pieces of doilies, cut paper, and crayons. Then display the decorated chart in your classroom for the duration of your animals-in-winter studies.

We live in Chicago. It is very cold and really windy a lot. Some of the birds fly away. Some of them stay and we will feed them at school.

Heading South

Youngsters will come flapping out of this idea with an impressive new vocabulary word and some solid science information. Begin by reading aloud Nancy White Carlstrom's *Goodbye Geese* (Scholastic Inc.) Then ask your little ones why they think the geese are flying south. After your discussion, explain that when fall temperatures begin to drop, some animals travel to places where the weather is warmer and food is easier to find. This type of traveling is called *migration.* Write the word on the board and find out if your children have ever seen geese that appeared to be migrating. The illustration in the book and the pattern on page 93 provide a springboard for discussing the *V* pattern in which the geese fly.

Migration In Motion

After introducing migration (see "Heading South"), do the following activity to bring home the whole migration concept. On a chilly day, designate an area of your playground to be "north" and your classroom to be "south." Have your youngsters pretend to be geese and "fly" to the north section of your playground. While they are in the north, encourage your little geese to waddle around among the flock. After a while, discuss the lack of food and the cold temperatures. Ask the geese where they could go to find food and warmth. Then have students arrange themselves in a *V* formation and fly back to your classroom—with sound effects, of course—where you have a little snack waiting for them.

Hibernation Day

Eyelids begin to droop...a yawn here and there...a child resting in a cozy curl-away corner. We all know that these phrases are not likely to be descriptive of the every-day early-childhood classroom. But maybe with this idea your youngsters will get a feel for the state of hibernation—if only for a few minutes! Introduce the word *hibernation*, and tell children that hibernation is a type of quiet sleep and rest that some animals enter during the winter. Hibernating mammals include chipmunks, ground squirrels, hedgehogs, wild hamsters, bats, and bears. Most of these animals eat large amounts of food in the fall; then find a sheltered place to sleep away the cold, winter days.

Then ask children what *they* do when the weather is particularly cold, snowy, or stormy. Guide youngsters to determine that, in a way, people hibernate too! Then plan a Hibernation Day at school. To prepare, have youngsters brainstorm a list of indoor activities that they enjoy. The next time a stormy day is predicted, have each child bring a favorite blanket or quilt and slippers to keep him warm and cozy. During the day, participate in the activities on your indoor-activities list, listen to music, share stories, and have some hot cocoa. When it's rest time, have each child pretend to be the hibernating animal of his choice and curl up in a cozy spot for a little winter's nap. Shhhhhh...there are kids trying to hibernate!

Saving For A Wintry Day

Scamper, scamper, scamper! What's all the fuss about? If you have squirrels in your area in the fall, set up a squirrel observation station. Stock the station with a supply of art paper and crayons. Ask youngsters to observe the squirrels and record (write/illustrate) their findings. Discuss children's observations; then find out if anyone knows what the squirrels are up to. After your discussion, share Brian Wildsmith's *Squirrels* (Scholastic Inc.) to determine exactly what those bushy-tailed fellows are doing.

Kids' Cache

Once your little ones have determined the purpose behind all that scampering about (see "Saving For A Wintry Day"), they'll be primed to do some fall gathering of their own. In advance, hide individually wrapped snacks and/or candies around your room (or around your playground, if appropriate). Review the gathering behaviors of squirrels; then encourage youngsters to pretend to be squirrels and gather all the hidden treats. Have your squirrels store the treats in a basket. Then—just when you need it in the dead of "winter"—return to your stash for a bite to eat!

Won't You Come For Dinner?

Although some birds migrate to warmer climates for the winter, many birds stay right where they are. Your youngsters will enjoy making bird feeders to give homebody birds a little wintry treat. Save milk cartons from school lunches until you have one clean, dry carton for each child. Cut the top off each carton as shown. Assist each child in punching randomly placed holes along the side panels of her carton. Also punch two holes on opposite sides near the top of the carton. Tie a length of yarn through the top two holes. Then create a perch by inserting a pencil through two holes on opposite sides of the carton. Fill the carton with birdseed; then hang it from a readily visible tree branch. Guess who's coming to dinner?

Give Me Shelter

Some familiar animals search out or build shelters that serve as warm, safe homes during the winter. Several different animals have unique homes that your youngsters can learn to identify. Reproduce the small animal patterns (at the top of page 92) and the animal-homes scene (on page 94) to make a matching activity for each of your youngsters. Have each child color each animal, cut it out, and glue it to the appropriate place on the animal-homes scene; then have him color the remainder of the page. Encourage the children to take their work home and share their knowledge about winter animals with their families.

Winter Wear

Brrrrrr! The temperatures are dropping and our furry friends need to bundle up. Some animals that have fur grow thicker, more protective coats to insulate them from the cold winter temperatures. And just like animals, *people* need to bundle up for winter, too! Share the following poem with your youngsters. When the children are familiar with the poem, ask each child to draw and color a picture of an animal in its winter coat. Next take a photo of each child wearing his own winter garb. Mount the picture next to that child's drawing. Have each child write/dictate to complete the sentences (see the illustration). Display the pictures and a copy of the poem on a bulletin board.

The fluffy red fox has a warm winter coat.
I can wear a red coat, too!
The fluffy red fox *needs* a warm winter coat,
Just like me and you.

The big black bear has a warm winter coat.
I can wear a black coat, too!
The big black bear *needs* a warm winter coat,
Just like me and you.

The frisky gray squirrel has a warm winter coat.
I can wear a gray coat, too!
The frisky gray squirrel *needs* a warm winter coat,
Just like me and you.

The old brown groundhog has a warm winter coat.
I can wear a brown coat, too!
The old brown groundhog *needs* a warm winter coat,
Just like me and you!

by Lucia Kemp Henry

Winter Weather Action Poem

Use this action poem to help reinforce some of the facts about animals in winter.

Winter is cold.
There is snow in the sky.
The squirrel gathers nuts
And the wild geese fly.

Hug yourself and shiver.
Flutter fingers above your head.
Pretend to gather nuts.
Flap arms.

The fluffy red fox
Has his fur to keep warm.
The bear's in her cave
Sleeping all through the storm.

Cup hands over head to form ears.
Stroke arms as if stroking fur.
Form a cave shape with your arms.
Fold hands under cheek and pretend to sleep.

by Lucia Kemp Henry

The bear has a brown coat.
Kevin has a blue coat.

The Literature Link

Wild Horse Winter
Written by Tetsuya Honda
Published by Chronicle Books

This fiction book packs in the facts. It intrigues children with the captivating account of the wild Dosanko horses found on the island of Hokkaido in Japan (see the editor's note at the end of the book). As you read aloud, stop where the text reads "Slowly, the night turned into morning." Invite children to examine the illustration carefully. Ask them what they think happened to the horses. Then finish reading the book

Encourage each child to create a construction-paper Dosanko horse. Glue all of the horses to a sheet of chart paper. Next cut a sheet of blue craft paper sized to fit over the chart paper. Use white paint to title the paper "A Blanket Of Snow." Arrange the blue paper in your art center along with a supply of doilies, white paint, sponges, and/or wide paintbrushes. Have each child use a sponge or paintbrush to stencil sections of doilies all over the blue paper. When the paper is fully decorated, staple the top of it over the chart paper. Encourage children to tell the story of the Dosanko horses to classroom visitors— then lift the blanket of snow to illustrate!

Whose Tracks Are These?
Written by Jim Nail
Published by
Roberts Rinehart Publishers

After sharing and discussing this clue book of familiar forest animals, why not keep on trackin'? Duplicate several sets of the track patterns (page 92) on white construction paper. Encourage children to color the tracks blue to simulate shadowed snow. Then have students cut out the tracks and glue them to one long strip of white bulletin-board paper. Display the finished project on a wall; then encourage children to identify what animals made which tracks. Then label the tracks if desired.

Here Is The Arctic Winter
Written by Madeleine Dunphy
Published by Hyperion Books For Children

Little ones wil enjoy this book with lyrical text and glowing illustrations. After sharing it, duplicate several sets of the Arctic animal silhouettes (page 96) on tagboard. Cut out the patterns; then place them in your art area along with blue construction paper, white tempera paint, and toothbrushes. Invite each child to create a snowy-day animal scene. Have a child choose one or more patterns that he would like to use. Instruct him to arrange the patterns on the blue paper. Then have him lightly dip a toothbrush into the white paint. Direct the child to hold the toothbrush and run his thumb along the toothbrush bristles to create a snowy effect. When the scene is as snowy as he likes, set it aside to dry. Later carefully remove the patterns to reveal a snowy animal scene.

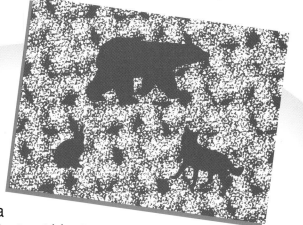

Small Animal Patterns
Use with "Give Me Shelter" on page 89.

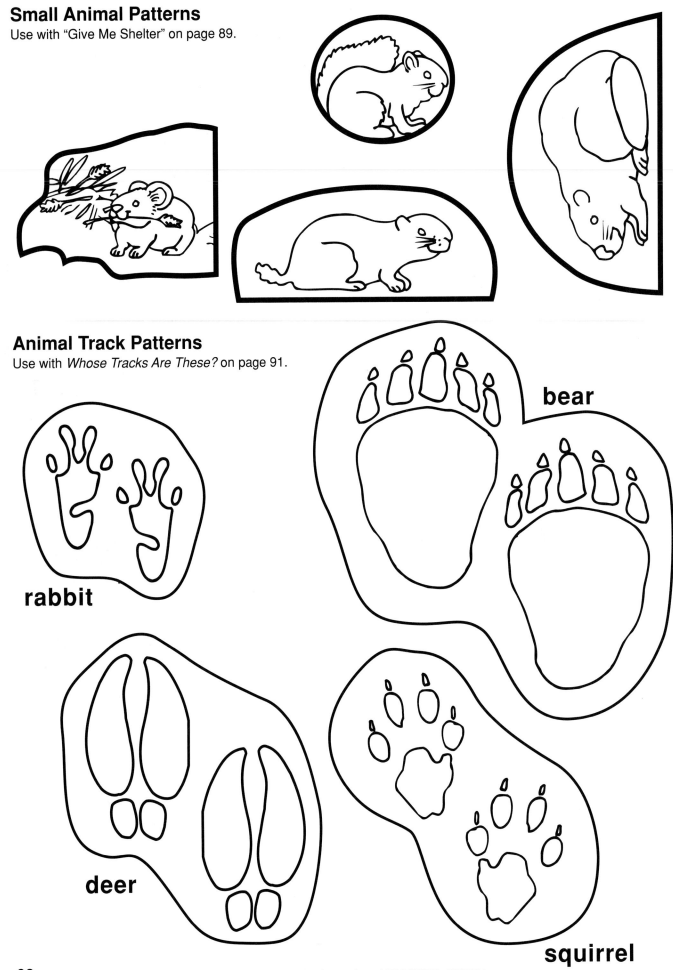

Animal Track Patterns
Use with *Whose Tracks Are These?* on page 91.

bear

rabbit

deer

squirrel

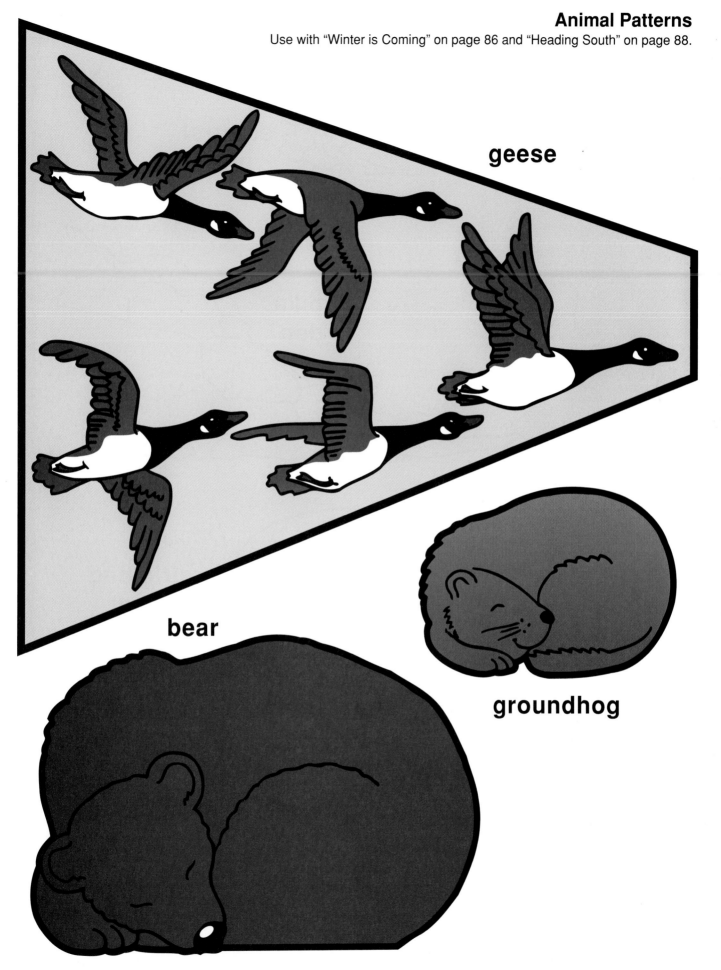

geese

bear

groundhog

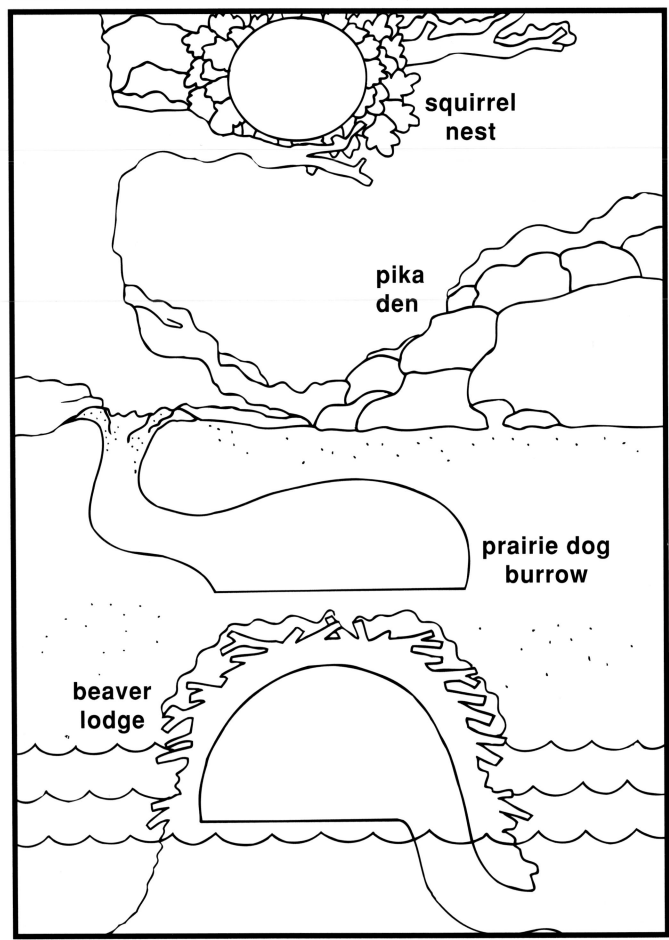

squirrel
nest

pika
den

prairie dog
burrow

beaver
lodge

squirrel

chipmunk

otter

fox

birds at the feeder

Arctic Animal Silhouettes

Use with *Here is the Arctic Winter* on page 91.

arctic wolf

arctic hare

caribou

arctic owl

polar bear